I0036868

Testimonials

Transforming Norm is a comprehensive guide for change leaders striving to make workplaces safer and more effective places to be. An essential guide for leaders wanting to influence positive change in the workplace.

—**Jonah Berger, Bestselling author of** *Contagious* **and** *The Catalyst.*

Tanya Heaney-Voogt is a passionate leader who supports organisations in building and sustaining mentally healthy workplaces. In *Transforming Norm*, Tanya provides practical, accessible and actionable advice to assist organisations in creating thriving and healthy working environments. This book is a must-read for leaders and HR and safety practitioners!

—**Georgie Chapman, Partner, HR Legal.**

Smart, clever and successful businesses are evolving the way they work. And they must. Old ways of working reveal the toxic traits, bad leadership behaviours and unhealthy cultures that are overdue for change. No additional growth or productivity is possible when the environments and situations people work in are unhealthy. This is not about buying new ergonomic chairs or running a few mindfulness workshops! The transformation required, needed and valued by employees is possible. In this thorough and helpful book, Tanya Heaney-Voogt steps through the requirements to create workplaces where people 'work well'. If you're a leader, proceed with caution if you don't have this book at your side. It's the perfect companion to healthy change and transformation for today's workplace.

—Lynne Cazaly, Keynote speaker and award-winning author on new ways of working.

This is a little gem of a book packed with insights, helpful hints and practical tools to help leaders at all levels create safer workplaces. Tanya challenges us to lead from the front and distils the critical concepts into an easy to read guide. This is a book to go back to over and over again as a must-have resource for leaders, managers, educators and businesses.

We must do better in creating psychological safety and reducing harm to our precious workforce. Tanya has provided a brilliantly simple blueprint to do so.

—Cayte Hoppner, Chief Operating Officer and mental health nurse.

Everybody knows that creating a mentally healthy workplace is important. The challenge is knowing where to start, how to overcome the many obstacles that get in the way and what to do in order to create real and lasting change. Thankfully, in *Transforming Norm*, Tanya speaks to all three. It's packed with helpful strategies and powerful questions to help create environments where people can truly thrive.

—Shane Michael Hatton, Author of *Let's Talk Culture*. www.shanemhatton.com

Transforming Norm

Transforming Norm

Leading the change to a mentally healthy workplace

TANYA HEANEY-VOOGT

Published by Tanya Heaney-Voogt

First published in 2022 in Melbourne, Australia

Copyright © Tanya Heaney-Voogt

tanyaheaneyvoogt.com

Melbourne, Victoria

The moral rights of the author have been asserted.

All rights reserved, except as permitted under the Australian Copyright Act 1968 (for example, fair dealing for the purposes of study, research, criticism or review). No part of this book may be reproduced, stored in a retrieval system communicated or transmitted in any form or by any means without prior written permission from the author.

This book uses stories to enforce the meaning behind relevant chapters. Permission to use these stories has been provided.

Every effort has been made to trace (and seek permission for the use of) the original source of material used within this book. Where the attempt has been unsuccessful, the publisher would be pleased to hear from the author or publisher to rectify any omission.

Edited by Jenny Magee

Designed, typeset and printed in Australia by BookPOD

ISBN: 978-0-6455002-0-2 (paperback)

ISBN: 978-0-6455002-1-9 (ebook)

NATIONAL LIBRARY OF AUSTRALIA

A catalogue record for this book is available from the National Library of Australia

This one is for you, JP, the most colourfully eloquent cage shaker I've had the pleasure to know.

Contents

Introduction

'On the whole, workplaces want to be mentally healthy but lack awareness of how to achieve this.'
— Australian Government Productivity
Commission report

What is a mentally healthy workplace?

There is still much confusion about what a mentally healthy workplace means.

For some, the phrase conjures up images of feet on the desk, sip-your-latte environments, absent of stress, accountability or responsibility. Others fear it is a workplace invasion into individual mental health.

In fact, it is none of those things.

A mentally healthy workplace is one that has recognised the role work plays in individual psychological wellbeing and chooses to take steps to enhance the positive and mitigate the negative.

It recognises that people are at the heart of its productivity and customer interactions and that a positive and safe workplace culture enables organisational success.

And yes, for some people, this is revolutionary thinking.

Fear-based leadership is still alive and well in many workplaces.

Decades may have passed since the Industrial Revolution, but some leadership practices and behaviours have not changed. Command and control styles, fear-based leadership and psychologically harmful behaviours are still alive and well in many workplaces.

> ## Fear-based leadership is still alive and well in many workplaces.

Therefore, it is not surprising to see an increase in work-related stress claims and billions of dollars of lost productivity in the Australian economy associated with mental ill-health.

These outdated ways of leading, these old-fashioned workplace norms, no longer serve us. Our people expect, and deserve, better.

The time has come to lead the change. To focus on safe and effective leadership, take strategic actions to transform the way we have always done things, and build new, more enabling, and psychologically safer cultural norms.

The case for change has never been more compelling.

Who is Norm anyway?

Norm *(noun): A standard, model or pattern. General level or average.*
— Dictionary.com

Social norms: *The unwritten rules of beliefs, attitudes, and behaviors that are considered acceptable in a particular social group or culture. These groups range from friendship and workgroups to nation-states.*
— Simplypsychology.org

Cultural norms: *The standards we live by. They are the shared expectations and rules that guide behavior of people within social groups.*
— Globalcognition.org

Social and cultural norms: *Rules or expectations of behavior and thoughts based on shared beliefs within a specific cultural or social group. While often unspoken, norms offer social standards for appropriate and inappropriate behavior that govern what is (and is not) acceptable in interactions among people.*
— National Academies Press[1]

Social and cultural norms are intangible, invisible beasts that can create amazing unity and harmony or be destructive and, in some circumstances, induce violence. Social norms are likely to be less regulated than workplace norms.

We all play a part in either setting and reinforcing or challenging and transforming accepted cultural norms.

Workplace culture has often been defined as 'the way we do things around here'. These can be spoken or unspoken pressures and constraints.

You will learn in the following chapters why it takes an integrated transformational approach to lead the change to a mentally healthy workplace and how we can challenge deeply entrenched unhelpful norms.

This book is in three parts, encompassing segments from the following Wheel of Change model. Each chapter represents an element necessary for transformation.

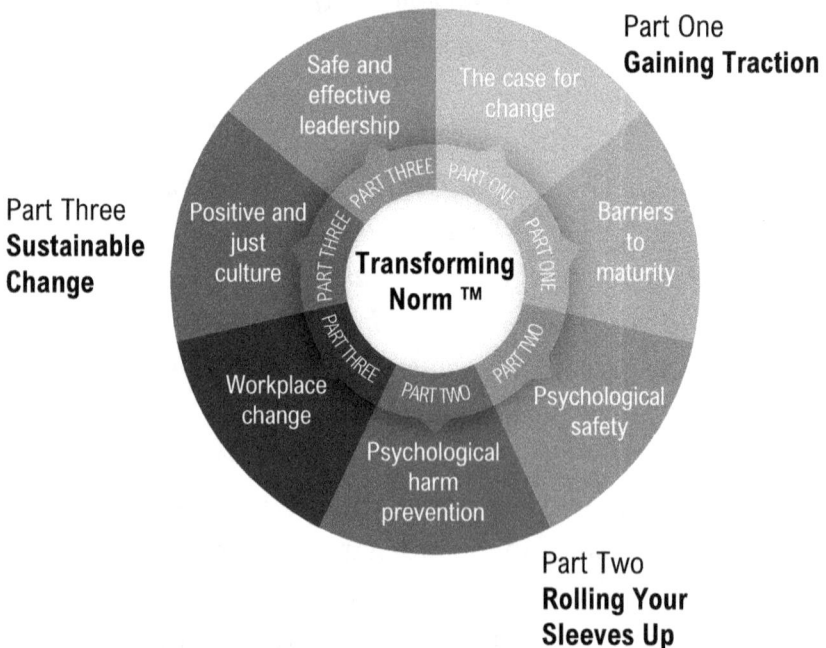

Part One
Gaining Traction

Safe and effective leadership

The case for change

PART THREE PART ONE

Part Three
Sustainable Change

Positive and just culture

PART THREE **Transforming Norm ™** PART ONE

Barriers to maturity

PART THREE PART TWO

Workplace change

PART TWO

Psychological safety

Psychological harm prevention

Part Two
Rolling Your Sleeves Up

Part One: Gaining Traction

This part takes you through the **case for change** and explores the **barriers** to progressing your transformational activities. Here you will find compelling statistics and practical strategies to mitigate the roadblocks that may be hampering your transformational journey.

Part Two: Rolling Your Sleeves Up

Part Two takes a deep dive into the specifics of transformational activities. We'll look at how to foster practices that create **psychological safety** and proactively mitigate the risks of **psychological harm**. This is the deep shift work required to transform outdated norms into more mentally healthy practices.

Part Three: Sustainable Change

Here we examine three areas that constantly shift and evolve in our volatile, uncertain, complex, and ambiguous (VUCA) world of work. They are **workplace change, positive and just culture,** and **safe and effective leadership.**

These ultimately shape how people work together and feel about their organisation. Your work here will determine the sustainability of your new norms.

We close out Part Three with specific guidance on leading the change to a mentally healthy workplace. You will learn how to engage your change cohort and communicate and initiate your transformation project.

Transformation is not linear. While I've ordered the segments in this wheel, you may (and likely will) dip in and out of them as your workplace needs dictate.

At the end of each chapter, you will find a summary reflecting the key points and a series of actions to help you Transform Norm.

Enjoy, dear reader, and keep leading the change.

Part One

Gaining Traction

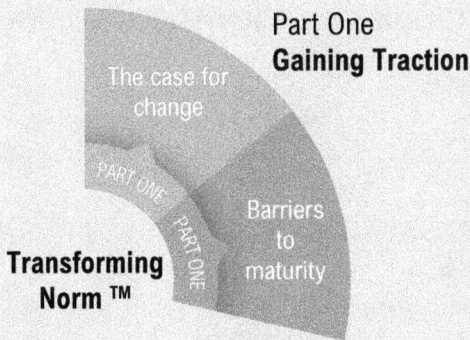

Chapter One: The Case for Change

Chapter Two: Barriers to Maturity

Chapter One

The Case for Change

Transformation takes time.

Work plays a significant role in most people's lives and positively or negatively influences mental wellbeing.

Before COVID, one in five adult Australians experienced a common mental illness such as anxiety or depression in any given year. It is anticipated these statistics have risen significantly due to the impact of the pandemic.

Organisations that are not mentally healthy risk contributing to additional rates of mental ill-health and exacerbating the severity for people with existing conditions.

In 2020, the Productivity Commission of Australia reported the estimated cost of absenteeism and presenteeism due to mental ill-health in Australian workplaces at AU$16.6 billion dollars per year.[2] When factoring in the lower participation rates of Australians due to mental illness, these estimations increase to AU$39 billion.

Workplaces are grappling with ways to support a tired and deflated workforce.

In the final report from the Inquiry into Mental Health, the Commission listed among its recommendations the need to 'equip workplaces to be mentally healthy'. It recommended that 'the same risk management approach applied to physical health and safety be applied, as a priority, to psychological health and safety'.[3]

COVID has shone a spotlight on psychological health and safety as nearly every Australian has felt the impact in some way.

Workplace conversations about mental wellbeing are now more open, or at least the language is being normalised, which is essential in this change journey.

Workplaces are grappling with ways to support a tired and deflated workforce. Some, such as frontline workers, are juggling intense workloads and health and safety risks, while others balance the challenges of working from home and a lack of separation between home and work.

Our front-line workers have done it very tough. In sectors already predisposed to high rates of occupational violence and aggression, this has increased along with work intensity, demands, and environmental challenges. The impact on workers was reflected in the AU$1.2bn loss reported by the Victorian WorkSafe agency in the 2020/2021 year (on the back of a $3.5bn loss the previous financial year).[4] The agency attributed this loss to escalations in mental injury claims which made up sixteen per cent of all compensable claims. WorkSafe predicts this figure will rise to thirty per cent within the next nine years. Front line and public sector workers are disproportionately represented in these numbers.

What will happen if workplaces don't change?

The great resignation

In 2021, print and social media were rife with fearful tales of mass resignations and crippled industries as workers left their workplaces in droves.

There are many reasons why this was not entirely unexpected. However, it's more useful to see it as an opportunity to transform workplace norms rather than buckle at the knees. It's a chance to focus on how to retain people rather than blame heightened turnover on some phenomenon you can't control.

> Foster the great retention.

There will always be natural attrition and movement. If your focus is on building and sustaining a positive, psychologically healthy workplace culture, then instead of fearing the great resignation, see it as an opportunity to foster the great *retention*.

Mentally healthy workplaces have a distinct competitive advantage. From an employee retention perspective, it's no secret that employees want:

- to work in an organisation that values, develops and supports them, not treats them as a commodity

- their thoughts and contributions to be recognised and appreciated, not disregarded or punished

- a psychologically safe environment that drives inclusion, learning, team performance and innovation, and

- workplace psychological hazards mitigated.

If your approach is transformational, not transactional, you are taking steps to build new workplace norms and champion retention.

A strategic approach

A mentally healthy workplace requires a strategic approach to transform how you have always done things and build new psychologically beneficial cultural norms. This work must be linked to the organisation's goals and objectives and involves developing a strategic action plan with executive (and often board) oversight and commitment.

The plan is monitored and reported, and resources are allocated to progress activities. Change messaging should make it clear that this is the way forward for the whole organisation.

Resist seeing this as purely an HR exercise. Ensure messaging from the top is about the new way of doing things across the entire organisation. Talk about *transformation* and support people through the change. More on this later.

The five integrated components

A mountain of empirical evidence[5] [6]indicates that a mentally healthy workplace is achieved through a planned and integrated focus on five key areas.

1. promoting psychologically safe practices and behaviours

2. proactively mitigating work-related stress factors that can lead to psychological harm

3. creating and sustaining a positive workplace culture

4. building safe and effective leadership practices, and

5. reducing the stigma around mental health to ensure people can obtain the support necessary to optimise their mental wellbeing and support for the unwell to stay or return to work (much as we do for physical health and injury).

Assessing your workplace maturity

Your future state vision will always be to embed mentally healthy ways of working into the organisation's fabric. Reflect on the model and table descriptors below to identify your current state. As you work through this book you will identify the specific activities that will progress your organisational maturity and transform your norms.

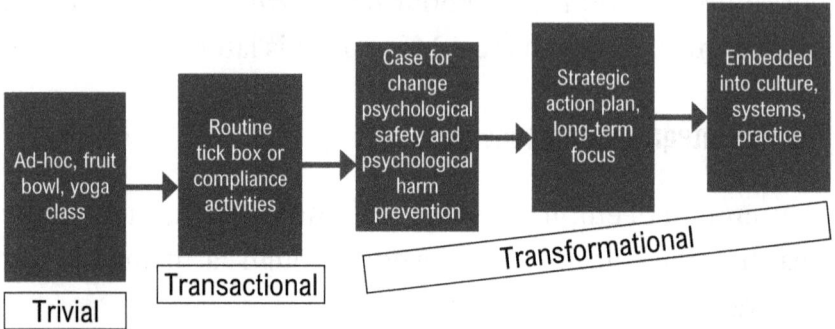

Figure 1: Mentally healthy workplace maturity model

Measuring maturity

In 2021 I did a presentation for the Australian Human Resources Institute Mildura Network on creating a mentally healthy workplace. In the midst of COVID, more than a hundred HR practitioners from across Australia registered for the event.

During the webinar, I asked attendees to rate their current level of organisational maturity against this model. Most were at the Trivial and Transactional stages, with one third at the Case for change (early transformational) and a few at the Strategic action plan development level (mid-transformational).

That reflects most workplaces I speak with, which tend to be in the early stages and recognise the need to move into the transformational space. They often need support to develop a business case and get traction at executive level.

Smaller workplaces tend to focus on trivial activities that are well-intentioned but ad-hoc.

All Australian public entities have a mandatory training program. Many rely on these activities to address factors such as bullying and harassment, discrimination and other legislative elements holding them in the transactional space.

Some sector peak bodies have released industry-specific wellbeing plans in efforts to engage their agencies in progressing transformational work. Still, many entities have given these a superficial focus or remain unsure of how to begin.

Few workplaces have finalised their Strategic action plans. Those that did (particularly those with plans in place before COVID) have seen enormous benefit and considerable staff re-engagement from their demonstrable commitment to making the workplace mentally healthier.

Where is your organisation at?

Use the following descriptors to understand where your workplace currently sits against the maturity model, then answer the reflection questions to identify your next steps.

Trivial	Transactional	Transformational
Well-intentioned but episodic Fruit bowl and yoga class type activities One-off No integrated focus on psychological wellbeing and harm prevention A potentially false sense of wellbeing, addressed through ad-hoc initiatives.	Compliance-based mandatory training programs. The focus is on completion rates, not changing behaviours. KPI-based for leaders, who are accountable for completion rates, rather than reviewing and monitoring behaviours that exhibit learnings. May be unsure how to progress in maturity or have leadership or cultural barriers.	Early May have a sector mental health and wellbeing plan they are responding to. May have wellbeing (broader sense) on the agenda. Starting to understand the impact of psychological wellbeing on employee engagement, workplace productivity and business outcomes. Starting to formulate or understand the business case for change beyond the OHS function. May be looking at proactive psychological harm prevention activities due to increased mental injury claims filed/upheld. May consider psychological safety training and deepening understanding of how this aligns with safe and effective leadership.

Trivial	Transactional	Transformational
		Mid Executive buy-in and understanding of the need for a long term focus on this work. Strategic alignment and action plan development with Executive +/- Board support. Clear resourcing across the organisation. Integrated transformation focus. Sits with all leadership, not just HR/OHS
		Advanced Well advanced, subsequent years of embedding new norms aligning to the five elements of a mentally healthy workplace. Active and relentless focus on maintaining the culture. Everyone's role and responsibility to ensure new norms are lived and valued. (Not set and forget)

When you consider the five elements of a mentally healthy workplace, what have you focused on so far? Where are the gaps?

Where does your organisation sit on the maturity levels?

Do you have a solid business case for change?

Do you need internal support or sign off, or has this been achieved?

What steps are next for you?

Chapter Summary

Most workplaces want to be mentally healthy but lack awareness of how to achieve this.

Strong evidence at state and national levels supports the need for workplaces to be more mentally healthy.

Mentally healthy workplaces have a distinct competitive advantage.

Workplaces have a unique opportunity to strengthen their attraction and retention of key talent through developing mentally healthy work practices.

A strategic, integrated approach focuses workplaces on transformational activities, not transactional.

Taking Action

Prepare a business case for change and start sharing data and trends regarding the impact of unhealthy norms on mental wellbeing in the workplace. You can access a business case from my website www.tanyaheaneyvoogt.com/resources and add information relevant to your workplace.

Share the maturity model with your executive and leadership teams and ask them to rate where they think your organisation sits on the scale and what barriers may prevent progress.

Establish a Workplace Mental Health and Wellbeing Working Group. We don't need another committee just for its own sake, but keep these actions separate rather than incorporate them into a broader wellbeing working group. Those groups often have a primary focus on individual physical health and fitness rather than the workplace's role in preventing psychologically harmful behaviours, systems and processes.

What Actions Will You Take?

1. _____

2. _____

3. _____

Chapter Two

Barriers to Maturity

In my work across organisations, I have identified six distinct barriers to organisations progressing this transformation work or maturing in line with the mentally healthy workplace maturity model. These are outlined in this chapter, along with tactics to address them.

To succeed, you must understand and address these barriers early, so they don't become permanent obstacles.

Barrier #1: Understanding the phrase 'mentally healthy workplace'

The term is broad, subjective and easily misunderstood, meaning different things to different people. Some see the link between physical and mental health and focus on exercise and nutrition programs. Others hone in on individual mental health and introduce mindfulness activities and yoga classes.

For those in the field, a mentally healthy workplace is one where there is a strategic, integrated approach to protect, promote and support employee psychological wellbeing. It is based solidly on research and empirical evidence.

Even with the right intent, workplaces struggle to locate, review and make sense of the wealth of available information. This has been a major barrier to change. No one has time to do the leg-work on a topic that is unfamiliar and, in some cases, hard to conceptualise in a compliance-heavy, resource-lean world with many simultaneous distractions.

It's one of the main reasons I have written Transforming Norm, as existing material is heavy reading, complex and vast. I know what it's like to want to move forward but with no time or mental space to absorb the array of information and frame it in a way that will sell it down the line. That's the reality of this work.

Throughout the book, I'll provide clarity on what it means to be a mentally healthy workplace and give you actionable steps to transform your organisation.

> Workplaces struggle to locate, review and make sense of the wealth of available information.

The title of this book was born out of the reality that this is not quick-fix work. To truly create mentally healthy workplaces, we need to transform the way we have always done things and create new norms. And that leads me to barrier number two.

Barrier #2: Transform, not transact

The second barrier is the realisation that this work is transformational, not transactional.

It is not about quick fix activities or mandatory training programs. Transformation takes long-term commitment and focus.

It is common to feel overwhelmed when digesting what is involved, leading to resistance from change leaders and those up and down the chain of command. After all, we live in a world of instant gratification, which stops us from thinking long-term. Anything that requires the long haul sets people back a step or two.

Despite this, you can take simple steps to make massive impacts, sustaining energy, enthusiasm and motivation for the path ahead.

This book is your guide as you undertake the longer-term transformational work. And because I know that short-term wins sustain motivation and momentum in large change initiatives, I've peppered the book with practical actions you can take now. These will make a difference and add immediate value while the big wheels are turning.

We live in a world of instant gratification, which stops us from thinking long-term.

Barrier #3: Lack of a business case for change

The good news (as you read in Chapter One) is that there is clear and compelling evidence to support your case for change. Part Two of the book offers other valuable statistics. Be strategic.

Identify what motivates the leaders who will authorise the business case.

Are they driven by *culture* (people, heart), *productivity* (outcomes, efficiencies, success) or *economics* (cost of absenteeism/presenteeism, WorkCover claims and premiums)?

These are three distinct arguments, and to influence change, you must know and be armed with information relevant to your audience's motivations. You may need to focus heavily on one, two or all of these elements for maximum effect, but mostly you'll know the focus of the person who needs to approve this work. You have probably worked with them for some time and understand their motivations.

> Identify what motivates the leaders who will authorise the business case.

If you need more assistance, there's a free downloadable business case whitepaper on my website www.tanyaheaneyvoogt.com/resources/. The paper addresses all three arguments and will help with content, data and references.

Barrier #4: Lack of change management skills and knowledge

Human Resource, Occupational Health and Safety, and Organisation Development staff generally lead these change projects. Yet, in my experience, there is often an absence of change management experience within these teams. The Change Lab 2020 Workplace Report[7] states that even though change is a constant in workplaces, many people are not supported to develop the skills they need to navigate change well.

> One of your best investments will be in skills development for your change leaders.

One of your best investments will be in skills development for your change leaders.

Transforming cultural norms takes project management, change management and executive support. In many cases, transitioning people through change will require shifts in beliefs and attitudes. The project teams need at least introductory level change management competencies to drive these changes effectively and efficiently.

Throughout the book, you'll find change tips and actions that support you and your teams to lead this work. However, I strongly encourage you to ensure that at least one person in the project team has undertaken change management training.

Barrier #5: It's not the organisation's role

Organisations often ask me about the role of the work environment in individual mental wellbeing. Surely personal circumstances are more relevant, and we have no control over that? It is a valuable and often pressing question.

The following model demonstrates the factors that broadly influence individual mental wellbeing.

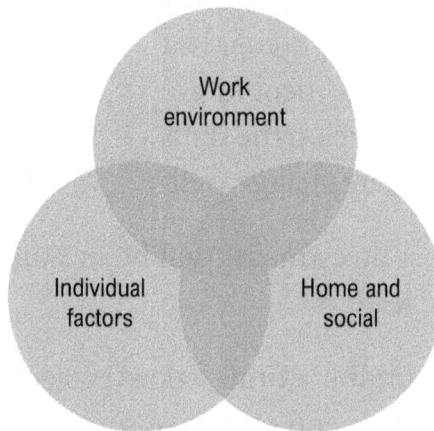

Figure 2: Factors influencing mental wellbeing

Unsurprisingly, all three factors are interconnected. Every individual is unique and complex, with their personality, personal history, beliefs, home and social aspects. Each plays a significant role in mental wellbeing, but the work environment also contributes to how individuals show up and respond and react to work events.

While we can't control what happens outside of work, we can influence these factors. And we have far more influence than we realise, as the following expanded models show. In these models, look for the activities that can contribute to dramatically enhancing the psychological wellbeing of your employees at work.

Work environment: full control

Nearly a quarter of Australian workers believe they have a mental health condition that work caused or made worse. That's one of the findings in the 2021 SuperFriend *Indicators of a Thriving Workplace* report.[8]

As a workplace leader, you have complete control over the initiatives, behaviours and practices you promote and accept.

That means total control to promote mentally healthy behaviours and positive workplace culture and complete control over how you support your employees to thrive at work. And for those who may be struggling, you govern how you can help them stay, or return, to work.

Employees spend most of their waking hours in the workplace, so it follows that it has a significant

Nearly a quarter of Australian workers believe they have a mental health condition that work caused or made worse.

impact on individual wellbeing. You can choose for this impact to be positive or psychologically unsafe. Whatever you decide, your team performance and business outcomes will directly correlate.

There are no excuses here. The buck stops with how leadership sets, models and enforces safe cultural norms. Yet more broadly, everyone in the workplace has a role in establishing and maintaining a positive and safe workplace culture.

While you only have total control over the work environment, you can heavily influence other factors that contribute to individual mental wellbeing.

Home and social environment: influence

COVID and home-based working have taken a toll on individual mental wellbeing. Some people have struggled with a sense of invasion into their home and private worlds through Zoom and Teams meetings, with camera access to real-time events. While this has been comical for some (who doesn't appreciate cats walking across screens?), it has provoked anxiety in others.

Working from home has put extra pressure on strained or unhealthy relationships, with reported family violence incidents increasing by 9.4% in 2020 to the highest on record, with 92,521 incidents.[9] It has also exacerbated environmental challenges, such as a lack of dedicated office space or room for a busy family.

Social factors are those things that affect the habits of individuals. They include relationships with our family, community, friends and associates, as well as our demographic, lifestyle, socioeconomic status, education levels and the support around us.

Despite the extra challenges in recent years, the workplace can positively influence employee home and social factors, for example, ensuring fair and equitable access to flexibility provisions and leave entitlements.

Work demands often create tensions at home.

Safe and effective leadership practices minimise emotional impacts on employees that can carry over into their home and social lives. Work demands often create tensions at home, so limited out-of-hours requirements can keep them reasonable.

Extra measures support employees in managing the pull between home and social factors and work. For example, the societal expectations on indigenous employees to attend 'sorry business' can cause internal conflict and angst. They stand to disappoint their workplace by requesting additional leave or their elders and the local community if they do not participate.

It leaves people in an unenviable position, and a growing number of workplaces now offer provisions for cultural leave to enable employees to balance these factors.

Such initiatives will help individuals manage the work, home and social interface and reduce work-related stress from the familiar conflict between expectations.

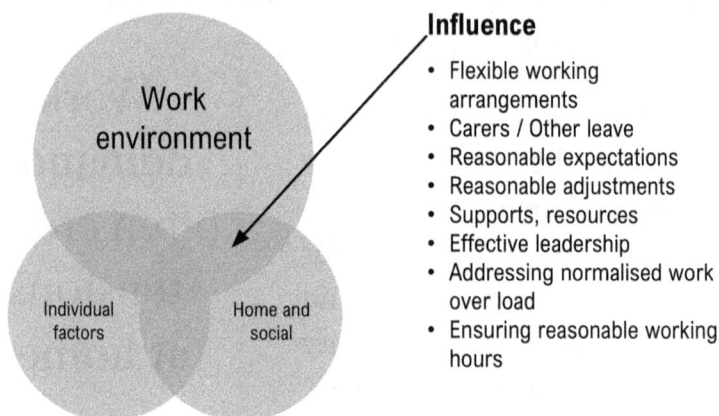

Influence

- Flexible working arrangements
- Carers / Other leave
- Reasonable expectations
- Reasonable adjustments
- Supports, resources
- Effective leadership
- Addressing normalised work over load
- Ensuring reasonable working hours

Work environment

Individual factors

Home and social

Figure 3: Work influence on home and social factors

Individual factors: influence

Individual factors are unique to each person. They include personality, beliefs, expectations, emotions, intellectual abilities, individual strengths and capabilities.[10]

While the workplace cannot control these factors, it can positively influence them by establishing systems and processes that enable people to function at their best. Fair and equitable application of policies and procedures (organisational justice), communicating effectively, supporting and communicating through change, ensuring jobs are designed to mitigate stressors (see Part Two) and providing appropriate support.

The workplace needs to develop safe and effective leaders with the skills and knowledge to coach, empower and grow individuals.

And finally, the workplace plays a significant role at this intersection by ensuring workplace culture is positive and just. In doing so, poor behaviours are less likely to trigger negative emotions and reactions in individuals.

Influence

- Coaching, reframing
- Leadership effectiveness
- Job design and control
- Organisational justice
- Change processes
- Communication and consultation
- Support and development

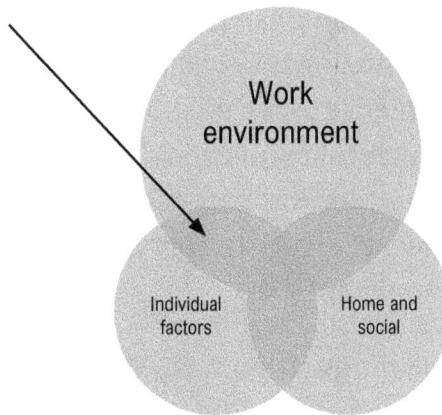

Work environment

Individual factors

Home and social

Figure 4: Work influence on individual factors

Barrier #6: People just need to be more resilient

It is rare to discuss influence factors without being asked about resilience. While it's a topic that fascinates me personally and professionally, it risks being flippantly applied or seen as a silver bullet in the workplace.

I'm sure you have heard, 'Oh, they just need to be more resilient'. Perhaps you've even thought or said it yourself? Or maybe you've felt you need to be more resilient to better cope with the demands of your workplace and workload. I know I have.

Resilience is a twofold concept, impacted by environmental (workplace, home, community, the world) and personal or intrinsic factors. I am often asked if sending employees to resilience training will help them cope better with their roles or a toxic workplace.

During a national presentation on occupational violence and aggression and its impact on staff emotional wellbeing, one attendee asked me how they could design a recruitment campaign that screened for appropriately resilient people. The question was well-meaning, with the ultimate intent of stopping the work factors impacting individuals — but it was the wrong question.

The better question was, why do organisations tolerate such damaging levels of behaviour from our customers? And, if we can't fix that, can we design the role, tasks, or a system to reduce the impact?

Sending staff to resilience training is not a panacea. It may help individuals develop or strengthen their personal strategies, but it does not absolve an organisation from the requirement to protect employees from psychological harm or provide the necessary prevention and support structures.

Building personal resilience: strategies, supports, resources and insights

Individuals can take steps to strengthen their resilience by creating a plan.

In the workplace, we can contribute to an individual's resilience by mitigating risks of psychological harm. We can look at job design and work-related stress factors and provide appropriate support, particularly at times of significant personal impact.

Sending staff to resilience training is not a panacea.

The SSRI model

To strengthen individual resilience, we need to identify the Strategies, Supports, Resources and Insights (SSRI) that we can draw from when needed. In professional resilience training, you are guided to develop your own SSRI plan.

It's a little confronting but also very reassuring, as it puts logic and systems into what is often an emotional space. Doing this in advance means we can draw on it when we cannot think logically or with a clear head. Developing an SSRI plan gives you the confidence to get through challenging times. I encourage you to do this — even superficially. Explore a resilience training program if you wish to formalise your approach.

As a leader, think about the strategies, strengths, resources, and insights you can draw on to support your employees. Work with other leaders to co-design an SSRI plan for your teams, divisions or the entire workplace.

The following template is adapted from an individual resilience plan. Use these examples as a guide, and co-design yours with your team.

SSRI	Reflection	Activity
Strategies Practical things we can do	What practical things can we do as a team when things go wrong or are challenging?	Team gathering Problem-solving approaches and mistake tolerance (psychological safety)
Strengths Drawing upon ourselves	What are the inherent strengths of the individuals and the team?	Undertake strengths-based assessments and map the team's strengths. Foster unity and increase self-efficacy and self-belief. Reflect on when we have made it through challenges before.

SSRI	Reflection	Activity
Resources Where we turn	Where can we turn for support and restoration when we are depleted and frustrated?	EAP services Workshops on wellbeing/psychological safety Coaches and mentors Teammates, relationships, laughter
Insights What we already know	How have we been inspired and motivated in the past? Inspirational sayings, motivation quotes. Useful perspectives or ideas	Coaching questions: Can you think of a time when we were challenged at work, and we got through? What did we do? What worked well for us? What new things can we implement this time? What are the opportunities for us in this challenge? How can we strengthen as a team to get through?

Chapter Summary

Barriers prevent workplaces from taking reasonable steps forward, and these need to be addressed to progress in maturity.

While individual and home/social factors influence how employees cope with situations at work, the workplace has a significant impact on the mental wellbeing of its employees and can control these factors. It can also strongly influence the interface between work and home and work and individual factors.

Sending staff to resilience training is not the answer and does not absolve an organisation from its OHS duties.

Taking Action

Develop a mitigation strategy to address the barriers in your workplace.

Start raising awareness of the intersections between work, home and social and individual factors and the aspects that the workplace (and leaders) can positively influence.

Ensure your change leaders and change team are equipped with basic knowledge of leading successful workplace change and overcoming change resistance.

Challenge assertions that people simply need to be more resilient with information that examines the factors of resilience and the workplace role.

What Actions Will You Take?

1. _____

2. _____

3. _____

Part Two

Rolling Your Sleeves Up

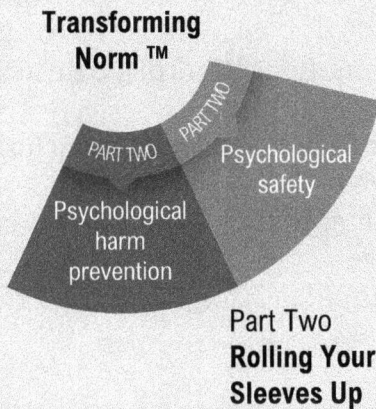

**Transforming
Norm ™**

PART TWO

PART TWO

Psychological
safety

Psychological
harm
prevention

Part Two
**Rolling Your
Sleeves Up**

In Part Two, we roll our sleeves up and get deep into the hard issues.

Chapter Three: Psychological Safety

Chapter Four: Psychological Harm Prevention Overview

Chapter Five: Unmanageable Workload

Chapter Six: Job Demand and Control

Chapter Seven: Poor Workplace Relationships

Chapter Eight: The State of Exclusion

Chapter Nine: Bullying and Discrimination

Chapter Ten: Mandatory Training Programs

Chapter Three

Psychological Safety

'A belief that one will not be punished or humiliated for speaking up with ideas, questions, concerns or mistakes.'
— Amy C. Edmondson, Harvard professor, author *The Fearless Organization*

' ... a social condition in which human beings feel (1) included, (2) safe to learn, (3) safe to contribute, and (4) safe to challenge the status quo — all without fear of being embarrassed, marginalized, or punished in some way.'
— Timothy R. Clark, author *The 4 Stages of Psychological Safety*

Understanding psychological safety

Psychological safety is a palpable feeling that everyone's voice matters, knowing that we can respectfully question and challenge to best achieve our organisational

> Psychological safety can be hard to define, but you know when things aren't right.

objectives. It is proven to be the single most crucial factor in high performing teams and is essential for preventing social context failures.

To understand the importance of the concept, we need to understand the history of psychological safety and the catastrophic failings that can arise when it is absent from the workplace. Psychological safety can be hard to define, but you know when things aren't right. Rather like workplace culture, it is almost intangible.

When environments are *not* psychologically safe, there's often a deeply troubling feeling — knowing that you can't make mistakes and you can never challenge the status quo.

Timothy Clark defines psychological safety as an environment of rewarded vulnerability.[11] In this context, vulnerability means taking an interpersonal risk.

Let's explore a story from one of my coaching clients to deepen our understanding.

Julie's story

Julie was a senior manager attending her first management team meeting in her new workplace. Twenty other managers were in the room, plus the executive members and the chief executive officer. But what surprised Julie most was the total lack of discussion and feedback from the management team.

A confident individual who had always been valued for her contributions in other organisations, Julie initially viewed the other managers as disengaged, disinterested and (if she was honest) ineffective.

The CEO was charming and engaging, and the executive often sought the managers' views during these meetings, but the management team rarely offered any thoughts or opinions. It was a static workforce, with long-tenured individuals, and Julie thought they perhaps just needed to move on.

As an energetic new member, Julie was keen to make a difference. She actively participated in the meetings sharing her thoughts and encouraging others to do so. At times, Julie was sure she caught knowing looks from some of the long-termers. Smug looks that said, 'Just wait. You'll soon find out'.

It didn't take Julie long to realise something was truly amiss. She began to hear stories of others who had tried and failed to make positive changes. Well-meaning colleagues gave her a friendly warning that challenging the status quo in that workplace was akin to career suicide. And a long line of people had gone before her.

Julie shook off the negativity, confident in her ability to influence. Her skills were recognised, and she started to climb the corporate ladder.

But that climb came to an abrupt halt when she spoke up to the executive about areas that required remediation if the organisation was to achieve its strategic objectives and re-engage the management group.

In hindsight, Julie told me the signs were obvious at that first meeting, but, as a natural optimist, she chose to ignore them. 'The reason there was utter silence in those meetings is that it was not safe to speak up. It was a fear-based culture where the only thing you were expected to say was 'Sounds great', 'I agree', and 'Yes, of course, you are awesome.'

She recalled that most of the executive did not want to discuss, collaborate or be challenged on anything. It was a command/ control environment. The meetings were more about lip service and the appearance of collaboration than genuine efforts to innovate and work together with experienced and senior workforce members. Julie felt it was such a missed opportunity for that workplace.

Psychologically safe workplaces value diverse thinking and invite contributions from all people.

Sound familiar? Julie's case is not unique. I regularly see and hear of similar environments. The ability to contribute to discussions or challenge ideas or how things have always been done is absent from teams and workplaces that are psychologically unsafe.

Psychologically safe workplaces value diverse thinking and invite contributions from all people. Unafraid to hear bad news, they are inclusive places to learn, where it is safe to contribute, offer your thoughts, solutions, and ideas and challenge the status quo.

Safe to be vulnerable

Essentially, these environments reward vulnerability, which we demonstrate every day by:

- revealing more of ourselves to our colleagues
- sharing our thinking on a problem or our ideas for improvements
- speaking up in meetings
- asking for help if we don't know how to do a task or want to learn more about something
- owning up to mistakes
- challenging the way things have always been done around here.

But we only do this if it is safe to do so. If we feel our vulnerability will not be punished.

Acts of punishment

Punishment can take many forms and be overt or covert.

Overt punishment can include obvious exclusion from groups, invitations, conversations, derogatory remarks and negative body language such as eye-rolling, smirking and head shaking.

> ## Covert punishment can feel like falling out of favour.

Covert punishment can feel like falling out of favour. It is often harder to prove and more akin to Julie's experience of 'career suicide' where career progression or promised opportunities vanish into thin air. It's a sense of falling out of favour or not being given the same options as others.

These are very real and common examples of environments that punish vulnerability.

The single most important factor

The term *psychological safety* was first coined in the 1960s when Edgar Schein and Warren Bennis recognised it as the means to support people through the uncertainty and anxiety of organisational change.[12] Sadly, for Schein and Bennis, poorly managed workplace change continues to be one of the leading work-related stress risk factors.

More contemporary work on psychological safety has been conducted by Amy Edmondson, the Novartis Professor of Leadership and Management at Harvard Business School and author of *The Fearless Organization*.[13] Edmondson is well known for her TED talks and her research on psychological safety and teaming.

However, the topic has really gained popularity since Google's famous Project Aristotle findings, published in 2016. That study identified that psychological safety is the single most important factor for high performing teams.[14]

> # Psychological safety is the single most important factor for high performing teams.

Beginning in 2012, Google's research team studied 180 teams to determine the recipe for creating high-performing teams. The researchers found that what mattered most wasn't who was on the team — it was how the team worked together.

Of the five key contributors to team effectiveness, researchers identified psychological safety as by far the most important because it enabled team members to feel safe to take risks and be vulnerable in front of one another.

They also found that individuals on teams with higher psychological safety:

- are less likely to leave
- are more likely to harness the power of diverse ideas from their teammates
- bring in more revenue, and
- are rated as effective twice as often by executives.

That, in itself, is a compelling business case, but there's more.

History is littered with examples where the lack of psychological safety led to diabolical events and consequences. Also known as *social context failures,* these events have cost lives and billions of dollars over recent decades, as stories in the following pages will show.

It can be life or death

In *The Fearless Organization*, Amy Edmondson explains that her discovery of the concept of psychological safety was almost accidental, when participating in a research study looking at medical error rates in hospitals.

Edmondson's role was to examine the effects of teamwork on medical error rates. Throughout the six-month study, team doctors, nurses and administration clerks completed diagnostic surveys, and direct team observation was undertaken.

Edmondson was delighted when the study results proved her hypothesis that there was a link between psychological safety and error rates. Yet the results confounded her. The team with the highest level of psychological safety also had the highest number of reported errors.

Fortunately, Edmondson did not rest there, conducting further research that ultimately proved that psychologically safe teams simply reported more errors than teams without the same levels of safety.

That is an important distinction. It is not that these teams make more errors. Instead, a spirit of openness and courageous curiosity makes them want to understand the reasons for the errors and make improvements. There is safety within the team to recognise the humanness of errors and safety to speak up and report. Commonly referred to as *mistake tolerance,* we encourage it by not punishing vulnerability when someone discloses a mistake.

If people are punished for mistakes, they are less likely to report them. There's great risk in this.

I delivered a psychological safety workshop to a team where one person shared that any reported mishap drew an automatic warning to the staff member involved.

As you will guess, I raised concerns about this approach. I suggested discouraging people from speaking up may prevent the organisation from addressing system or behaviour failings and cause more serious events. There was obviously historical context behind this practice, yet by having open conversations about psychological safety, you can deepen or re-examine thinking and decide to change practices to be more mistake tolerant.

NASA and social context failures

In 1990, after fifteen years of research and development, the Hubble telescope was launched by NASA's astrophysics division at the cost of US$1.7bn.[15] Now, if you're into astrophysics, you'll be all over what happened next, but read on if you don't leave earth that often.

Much to NASA's embarrassment, the telescope was launched with a flawed mirror that ultimately made the telescope useless. It was a minor defect that could have been easily rectified if the contractors had raised it.

The incident review board found that many tests before the launch would have identified the flaw. Yet the contractors feared raising the potential problem due to a demanding and inflexible schedule and budget constraints along with pressure and intolerance from the NASA team.

A root cause analysis of this event essentially declared *social context* as the main factor. That means the causes are social or psychological, or, in other words, interpersonal. The cost to NASA was far greater in reputation loss and political fallout.

This failure only cost money — not lives as in the Challenger and the Columbia disasters — both of which were also attributed to social context failures

Unseen and unmanaged social contexts

The space shuttle Columbia disintegrated as it re-entered the earth's atmosphere in 2003, killing all seven of its crew. In 2008, NASA's Stephen Johnson (Analysis Lead for Mission and Fault Management) wrote, 'Frequently, we find that the failure effects and cause are technical, but the root causes and contributing factors are social or psychological'.[16]

These social contexts determine how well teams work together to deliver organisational outcomes. There are many lessons to be learned from these stories and many more examples to draw on.

Whether launching a space shuttle or delivering a service or product, we need teams to work together effectively and not fear raising concerns due to demanding schedules and budget pressures or intolerance from leadership.

So how can you foster psychological safety in your teams?

Building psychological safety

In 2020, Oxford-trained social scientist and researcher Timothy R. Clark developed a model which brought tangibility to the concept of psychological safety.[17]

Building on the work of Edmondson, and Edgar and Schein, Clark developed the Four Stages model, providing a structured approach that would enable psychological safety to be easily understood and implemented in teams and organisations.

Let's unpack those stages.

The Four Stages model

As our earlier definitions have described, Clark defines psychological safety as a social condition in which all human beings feel:

- included
- safe to learn
- safe to contribute, and
- safe to challenge the status quo.

All without fear of being embarrassed, marginalised or punished in any way.

Clark's four stages comprise Inclusion safety, Learner safety, Contributor safety and Challenger safety. He says these stages are sequential, meaning you cannot achieve Challenger safety (the zone in which teams ideate and innovate) unless you have built the previous three.

The model resonates with leaders at all levels. During training, I take leaders through it using reflective questioning techniques to deepen their understanding of the concepts. Explored this way, the concepts are easily felt — and nothing fuels change faster than emotion.

Clark's model gives tangibility to the concept of psychological safety along with a staged approach for implementation.

If you reflect on the maturity model in Chapter One, you will note psychological safety sits in the early transformational stage.

Creating psychological safety takes patience and commitment. You won't always get it right, but there's power and growth in retrospective learning, reflecting on an event and recognising that you could have done something different to help foster a stage.

Let's examine the four stages.

Inclusion safety

Clark believes every human being has a basic human need to be included. He says this should be owed to all human beings regardless of any factor — unless there is a direct threat of harm. I wholeheartedly concur.

When have you felt excluded from a group or activity?

One of the common risks of exclusion I observe in offices is the coffee run. While virtual work has killed that off somewhat, how often have you experienced someone running out the door to the café while asking a few of their nearest and dearest if they want a coffee? It's loud enough for everyone to hear, but only a select few get asked.

When have you felt excluded from a group or activity?

Okay, in this scenario, I know you're damned if you do and damned if you don't. Many people don't ask widely because the five-minute dash risks turning into a marathon where you have to hire a minivan to cart back orders that went from three cappuccinos to a hazelnut shot latte extra hot with almond milk (but the barista won't do extra hot because that's not how 'real' coffee is made), a chocolate-free hot chocolate with marshmallows (but only if they're the 'fluffy ones' not the cheap plastic ones), a vanilla chai soy latte (but only if its the powder in the orange tin) and a no-fat, carb-free, faux choc chip muffin ...

But consider the new starter, fresh on board and sitting next to the nearest and dearest of the café runner (who, most sensibly, did not ask everyone for their orders).

While most of us can logically appreciate that you can't really ask *everyone* in the office, this behaviour clearly says an exclusive clique lives here. And you aren't part of it because you'd be asked if you were.

Challenge junk theories and shut down exclusive cliques.

Inclusion safety is about teams being mindful of the perception or reality of exclusive cliques and behaviours and our own conscious or unconscious sense of superiority.

Clark refers to these as 'junk theories of superiority'. These are the various ways we compare ourselves to other human beings and rate ourselves as better. A better car. A better home. A better neighbourhood. Race. Gender. Socioeconomic background. Sexuality. A role. Our title. Longer tenure. More popular. Thinner. Prettier. The list goes on. We all do it.

The trick is to challenge junk theories and shut down exclusive cliques as they occur. Become conscious of them and identify with each other on a human level — not superiority.

Exploring inclusion safety in depth is enormously beneficial to diversity and inclusion strategies, reducing the risk of discrimination, bullying and harassment and fostering a positive and safe culture.

In a leadership development workshop, I asked local government leaders to identify ways they could be more inclusive across their entire workplace, not just in their teams.

Here are some of the ideas they came up with.

- Be proactive and mindful to stop and introduce ourselves or the whole team to new starters.

- Find common ground with people and get to know them.

- Make sure we are saying simple good mornings and goodbyes.

- Make more effort to include and reach out to casuals.

- Put faces to names in the induction handbook.

- Introduce yourself to people you don't know.
  (In large organisations, you walk the halls with colleagues whose names you don't even know. Stop and say 'Hi' next time).

Have you noticed just how simple these strategies are?

Just because it's simple doesn't make it ineffective

I was recently reminded of the connection between simplicity and effectiveness when I commented on a social media post that said, 'To improve your wellbeing, rest more'. (This was in the context of wellbeing for business owners, not promoting physical inactivity.) I loved its simplicity. It was just so true.

> Lack of greetings or basic civility was the catalyst for problems.

The same philosophy applies to the inclusion safety suggestions described above. You might have scoffed at the simplicity of saying good morning or goodbye, but I can not tell you how many people I have coached, how many teams I have worked with, how many organisations have asked me to help turn around their worrying culture. And many have identified that a lack of greetings or basic civility was the catalyst for problems.

Truly.

So please, do not underestimate the power of a leader stopping to say good morning or goodbye to staff at all levels and tenures. It's powerful.

It's the same for the other suggestions. Imagine new hires getting a pleasant smile and a hello, or an introduction from a staff member in a different area. Or a leader?

I mean, how would it make you feel? Seen? Important? Valued? Included.

Each of these strategies can be replicated in a virtual or hybrid environment. If there's a face you don't know on Zoom or Teams, send a chat message to introduce yourself or book a virtual coffee chat. If you're leading the virtual meeting, do a meet and greet or a 'what's your favourite takeaway?' activity to create connections amongst the attendees.

Mistakes happen whether we like it or not.

There are myriad ways you can boost inclusion safety. But first and foremost, watch for behaviours and actions that exclude.

Learner safety

The second stage of psychological safety in Clark's model is the safety to learn. Amy Edmondson's work also heavily influences my activities in promoting learner safety in organisations.

The reality is that all human beings make mistakes, but when we're unsafe, we are more likely to cover these up for fear of persecution or humiliation.

Mistakes happen whether we like it or not. Don't punish people — help them learn. Enabling learning from events provides an opportunity to foster development and growth and correct systems and knowledge that may contribute to errors.

A psychologically safe environment rewards vulnerability rather than punishes it.

When I talk about this in workshops, I pause here. The issue of *mistake tolerance* often has people shifting uncomfortably and my fellow perfectionists twitching. Please accept that we all make mistakes. And it's okay. (If you're still twitching, I suggest you obtain a copy of Lynne Cazaly's fabulous book *Ish*.[18] It's a game-changer).

Yes, okay, sometimes the consequences of one little mistake are catastrophic. That's why having an environment where it is safe to learn is so important.

You don't punish someone's vulnerability if they make a mistake. You help them to learn, so they don't repeat it. If the same person continues to make the same mistake after many supportive efforts to clarify steps, processes and expectations, then you have a different problem.

Psychological safety is not about tolerating the same mistake being made repeatedly.

When talking about this, I often think about my typing prowess. I can churn out 100 words per minute with 98% accuracy when alone, but when someone stands over my shoulder, my fingers turn into footballs. The irony is that we all tend to make more mistakes when people watch our every move. If you want to explore this phenomenon further, read *The Inner Game of Tennis* by Timothy Gallwey.[19]

Shift the focus from what went wrong to what we have learned.

In the workplace, this hypervigilance is psychologically unsafe, so unless you're training a neurosurgeon who's practising on a real person, there's no need for it. Instead, focus on creating a safe place to learn. Don't shame or humiliate people if they make an error, approach it as a learning opportunity and help them grow.

Reflect on the events outlined earlier in this chapter. What would be different in these scenarios if people felt safe disclosing mistakes or reporting incidents?

Is it safe to learn and make mistakes here?

Have you ever felt unable to ask for help or too scared to admit you didn't know an answer to a question in your team or workplace? What about making a mistake and covering it up?

To learn and grow, we need to know there is a safe learning environment. In *The Fearless Organization*, Amy Edmondson says we need to frame execution problems as learning opportunities.[20] Shift the focus from what went wrong to what we have learned. Try this approach in your next meeting where a mistake is discussed. Remove blame and focus on curiosity and learning.

Contributor safety

Leaders are essentially the traffic controllers of their teams. They give the green or red light for individuals to contribute.

According to Timothy Clark, when a leader has established inclusion and learner safety, they can unleash the full potential of individuals by giving them permission to contribute.

> Teams and workplaces without contributor safety face an uninspiring future.

Encouraging contributions from your team means making it safe and inviting people to share thoughts, ideas and opinions on work issues. Permission to contribute is about team openness and respect. Leaders give this permission through open invitations and constructive responses — even if an idea isn't on the mark. Contributor safety in a team brings true collaboration, engagement, confidence and risk-taking.

If the leader keeps the red light on, does not invite, or even shuts down contributions, they extinguish the potential of individuals (and therefore the entire team), as the model in figure 5 shows.

There are catastrophic consequences for leaders who keep the red light burning bright. With individual potential extinguished and dealing with rejection, teams start to compete for favour. Fear permeates the group, meetings are silent, and conflict arises. The outcome is a team of guarded individuals who are just going through the motions. They are compliant rather than emotionally invested and bringing their all — a team with heightened psychological harm risks.

This environment, unsurprisingly, stifles creativity. There can be no innovation without creativity, fuelled by the diversity of thought, trust, and ideation.

Teams and workplaces without contributor safety face an uninspiring future. They lose their market competitiveness, have no attractive employee value proposition, and, at best, they stagnate.

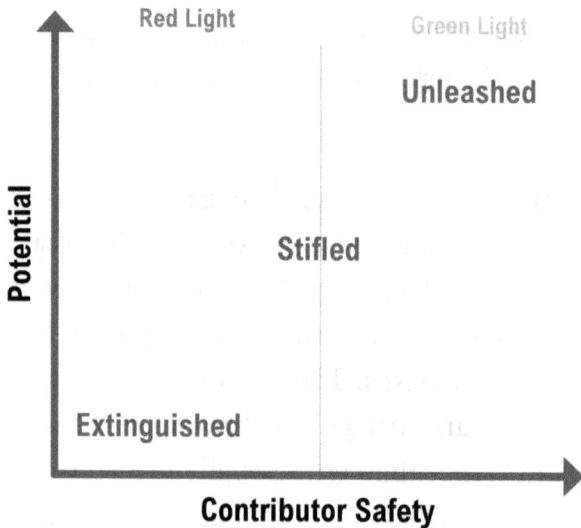

Figure 5: Unleashing potential

Imagine Isaac Newton returning from eating his lunch under the tree and telling his team he'd watched an apple fall and had thus discovered gravity. A red light leader would roll their eyes and walk off. A green light leader would take a seat and say, 'Tell me more.'

Don't assume people feel safe to contribute. You may not be shutting down contributions, but are you openly inviting them? Leaders should make it clear they welcome new ideas, potential solutions and fresh thinking and encourage individuals to bring those forward.

Challenger safety

How do you respond if someone on your team challenges your point of view or idea?

It's not always easy, right? And yes, it also depends on the tone and your relationship with that person. All these factors have a bearing on how you respond.

It can certainly take courage and confidence to reframe your fear and respond with curiosity — to be open to another's views and ideas and release attachment to your own.

In the workplace, leaders need to do just this and encourage this level of challenge within the team to get the best ideas, innovation and performance.

Leaders must be prepared for (and encourage) people to challenge them.

Accepting 'the way things have always been done around here' is lazy leadership. We need to challenge the status quo to refine our thinking, evolve and make the best of the diverse team contributions.

Timothy Clark says that one of the ways to foster challenger safety is to *assign dissent*. Allocating a specific team member the role of challenging a proposed action or decision means this person is not taking an interpersonal risk but has been given permission to challenge. It's a good way to remind your team that challenging is acceptable.

> Accepting 'the way things have always been done around here' is lazy leadership.

But, if you do not have this skill in your leadership group, consider the following activity.

Try on another hat for size

De Bono's *Six Thinking Hats* is an excellent strategy for leaders to embrace different views.

Edward de Bono was a leading authority in creative thinking and innovation and the direct teaching of thinking as a skill. Born in Malta in 1933, de Bono passed away in 2021, leaving an incredible global legacy and more than seventy published books. He is particularly well-known for his *Six Thinking Hats* model.[21]

Using this technique, groups approach a problem wearing various (metaphorical) hats to explore a problem and challenge thinking from all angles. The six hats are colour-coded and have assigned roles. They are:

- The White Hat: Facts, just the facts
- The Yellow Hat: Optimism, the benefits with a positive lens
- The Black Hat: Risks, difficulties, problems. The most powerful hat and problematic when overused. This hat finds all of the things that might go wrong, why something might not work
- The Red Hat: Feelings, intuition, hunches, gut instinct. The emotional hat that may share fears, likes, dislikes

- The Green Hat: Creativity. Looking at the possibilities, the alternatives and new ideas. An opportunity to ideate and share new concepts and perspectives.

- The Blue Hat: Controls the thinking process. This hat is the control mechanism to ensure that the Six Thinking Hats process guidelines are followed.

While I think there's merit in assigning a different hat to each team member, de Bono later advised that this was not how he intended the tool to be used. His idea is that the team views the problem from each of the various hat perspectives. For example, the group looks at possibilities with creativity (Green Hat), then with their gut instincts and emotions (Red Hat), and so on.

Undertaking this kind of activity encourages contributions and helps individuals challenge their viewpoints and appreciate diverse perspectives.

Why do we need to be challenged?

History is littered with corporate, environmental and human disasters traced back to despotic leadership practices and psychologically unsafe environments that deterred people from speaking up.

The greatest tragedy lies in the unrealised brilliance of organisations whose leaders are too entrenched in doing things the way they've always been done. They remain blinkered to the creativity and brilliance of those around them.

Chapter Summary

Psychological safety is proven as the single most important factor in any team.

Social context failures are a significant risk to workplaces.

Foster inclusion safety within your work teams as the foundational step to building psychological safety.

Challenge your own – and others – junk theories of superiority.

Make it safe to learn and work towards mistake tolerance. Remember, mistakes happen whether we like it or not, so wouldn't you rather know about them?

Acts of punishment can be overt and covert.

Avoid extinguishing the potential of employees by shutting down contributions.

Taking Action

Create awareness of what psychological safety means.

Share the language and intent to be more psychologically safe in your workplace, starting with inclusion and learner safety.

Look for concerning patterns where vulnerability is punished and seek to rectify those behaviours. For example, if people are shut down or their ideas are ridiculed in a meeting.

Work at the team, division or leadership level and explore ways to be more inclusive.

Help people resonate with the term *inclusion* by asking them to reflect on a time when they felt excluded from a group or event.

Talk about mistake tolerance and discuss what that may look like for your organisation and your context.

Try parallel thinking as an activity to foster contributions and make challenging safer.

Roll out psychological safety training to the people leaders in your organisation.

What Actions Will You Take?

1. _____

2. _____

3. _____

Chapter Four

Psychological Harm Prevention

A primary objective of a mentally healthy workplace is to protect your workers from psychological harm. While this has always been a legislative requirement, workplaces struggle to take proactive steps to mitigate work-related stress risks that can lead to psychological injury.

In this chapter, you'll find out why. While the terminology is a veritable minefield, we must be clear about what we are trying to achieve. There are common work-related stress risks, and Chapters Five through Eleven are a deep dive into the areas I encounter most frequently. We'll explore

Don't wait until something goes wrong.

how some of these risks arise and provide guidance on how to reduce or eradicate them. Taking a proactive approach is the key. Don't wait until something goes wrong. Identify these risks in your workplace and take steps now to prevent the impact.

The proposed Victorian OHS regulation amendments (to come into effect July 1 2022) will require workplaces to proactively identify and in some cases, create intervention plans for certain psychosocial hazards.

But first, a little bit of sensemaking.

Sensemaking

Like me, you may have been somewhat confused by all the terminology.

Across the wellbeing and legislative industries, there are a plethora of terms that seem, at times, to be used interchangeably. (And yes, I'm sorry, I'm also guilty of this). While OHS specialists tend to be clear on the terminology, many of those leading change within workplaces are baffled by the array of terms that seem the same – but are different.

I want to be completely clear about the terms I use and those you are likely to see elsewhere, so we're all on the same page when discussing this concept of psychological harm prevention.

The most common terms:

- psychological health and safety
- psychological harm prevention
- psychological hazards
- psychological injury
- psychosocial hazards

- work-related stress hazards/risks/factors

- mental injury.

All these terms are essentially in the same family. Technically though, psychosocial hazards are things in the design or management of work that can increase the risk of work-related stress. When excessive or prolonged, work-related stress may lead to psychological (or mental) harm or injury.

In my quest to keep things simple (and at the risk of staunch objections), I use the terms psychological harm risks or work-related stress risks to describe these things.

Don't get hung up on the terminology. Stay focused on what we are all trying to achieve, which is preventing work-related issues from impacting people psychologically.

> Don't get hung up on the terminology.

One last thing.

It is not uncommon for people to think that psychological safety (covered in Chapter Three) is merely the absence of psychological harm, but it's not quite that simple. For example, a workplace could technically have identified psychological harm risks and put mitigation strategies in place but still not have high psychological safety.

There's a definite intersection, but think of it this way:

Psychological safety is what you want to build, foster, and nurture in your workplace.

Psychological harm risks are what you want to identify, remove or mitigate.

The current state of norm

Organisations have long had the same OHS legislative responsibilities for both *psychological* and *physical* harm prevention — the requirement to proactively identify and mitigate hazards, and protect employees from harm.

In organisations of low maturity, most proactive activity tends to be transactional and centres around an annual mandatory training program (see Chapter Ten for more on these).

However, the escalating cost of mental injury claims supports the need for a proactive transformational approach to psychological harm prevention — not a transactional one.

The current state

In New South Wales, between 2014/15 and 2018/19, mental injury claims rose by 53% compared to 3.5% growth in physical injury claims. In 2018/19, 1.2 million workdays were lost to psychological injury.[22]

In response to this, SafeWork NSW developed its *Code of Practice: Managing Psychosocial Hazards at Work* which was released in May 2021.[23] It was the first State code of its type.

In Victoria in 2021, mental injury compensation claims rose to 16%, with WorkCover expecting this to increase to over 30% within the next decade.[24] There are now proposed psychological health amendments to Victorian Occupational Health and Safety regulations 'to strengthen the occupational health and safety (OHS) framework and provide clearer guidance to employers on their obligations to protect workers from mental injury. They will also reiterate that hazards that pose a risk to psychological health are as harmful to workers' safety and wellbeing as physical hazards'.[25]

Consider this alongside the case for change in Chapter One.

Think about the future of our workplaces.

What will happen if we don't change?

Hearing from the experts

I had the pleasure of interviewing Alexandra Rowe and Georgie Chapman to capture and share their expert insights.

Alexandra Rowe is the State Inspector of Operational Practice at SafeWork NSW. She was previously an Assistant State Inspector in the Psychological Health and Safety team responsible for developing the new Code of Practice and has investigated countless workplace matters and incidents concerning the management of psychosocial hazards.

Georgie Chapman is an HR lawyer and partner at HR Legal in Melbourne. The firm supports workplaces in establishing best practice processes to reduce the likelihood of psychological injury claims or grievances.

These experienced individuals share their insights throughout this section as we explore the barriers to being proactive and the common psychological harm risks we observe across workplaces.

Take note of their expert observations, as they may well help keep your employees psychologically healthy and keep your business out of trouble.

What does it mean to be proactive?

From a mentally healthy workplaces perspective, it means the following.

- Workplace actions and everyday behaviours align with your policy statements and the content of your mandatory training videos.

- Positive culture, psychological safety, psychological harm prevention and the importance of leading safely and effectively are discussed at regular meetings.

- Training and skills development initiatives are in place to build leadership efficacy and create awareness of work-related stress risks and the role of every leader and employee in preventing and mitigating these risks.

- Organisations plan strategically to traverse the maturity continuum. They identify the case for change and drive programs that create awareness of mentally healthy ways of working and how to achieve this in their context, focusing on strategic and sustainable integrated actions.

- Organisations actively challenge and rewrite unhealthy cultural norms and expectations to ensure the environment is conducive to sustainable, psychologically healthy employment.

More simply, it means preventing issues before they occur instead of waiting until a mental injury occurs and going through standard processes to investigate and report on that action.

Resistance is futile

Why do organisations resist shining a proactive light on psychological hazards? There are five reasons. Which of these resonate with your workplace?

Head in the sand

Georgie Chapman says 'head in the sand' is still the primary barrier. She says that traditionally we've thought of occupational health and safety as physical safety, whereas it always includes psychological health under current legislation. We've avoided dealing with it directly because of continuing stigma and discomfort.

> Prevent issues before they occur instead of waiting until a mental injury occurs.

Georgie says the central issue in workplaces is failure to take action. There's no perfect way to approach psychological health and safety and address the risks, but doing nothing is an obvious failure. As she comments, 'Many safety authorities have been actively building their resources and ranks to specifically address mental health hazards. This is remarkable because it demonstrates the shift in expectations from the regulator and the community in how we recognise and address mental health in the workplace.'

> # Doing nothing is an obvious failure.

Alexandra Rowe says workplaces struggle to know where to start and that so many of the workplaces she visits ask, 'What do I need to do? Just tell me what to do, and I'll do it'. It is one of the reasons why the NSW Code of Practice came into being; to provide more prescriptive and practical guidance for workplaces on how to identify and manage psychosocial hazards.

Stigma and myths

I believe stigma still exists, and there are many myths about mentally healthy workplaces.

The myths I hear most often are that the manager needs to assume a pseudo-counselling role or that workplaces need to accept poor productivity or under-performance from a worker who has a declared (or suspected) mental health condition.

Neither of these is true.

When you know that many adult Australians in any given year have a common mental health condition such as anxiety or depression, you will understand that these people can function at the very highest levels.

Myth-busting is important as you implement this work.

I asked Georgie Chapman whether she believes there's still some confusion or an attitude that people's mental health is just their problem at home. 'Yes, absolutely', she said. 'We have privacy obligations in workplaces, and when we're collecting health information, there are more stringent legislative protections. But there's a continuing stigma in our community around mental ill-health. Because of that stigma, people have been reluctant to speak up when they're experiencing it, which means (workplaces) haven't asked the question.'

There's a high risk for people to declare a mental health condition or a serious mental illness at recruitment for fear of discrimination. You can appreciate why, given the continuing stigma.

Similarly, if you are an existing employee in a working environment that does not show awareness, support or even tolerance for mental health, you are unlikely to admit you are struggling for fear of reprisal.

Ensuring psychological wellbeing is part of a leader's role.

Alexandra Rowe says it is not uncommon for business owners or divisional leaders to feel that they don't need to do anything about employee mental wellbeing. Alexandra says she often hears the comment, 'I'm not a psychologist'. She says leaders want to focus on running the business or the department and don't see psychological wellbeing as part of their role.

A silver lining

Georgie and I spoke of a positive side to the pandemic. It has provided an excellent opportunity for organisations to start having conversations about mental wellbeing — particularly where this has never been raised.

Many people had never experienced or been around anyone with a mental illness or challenges to their mental health. The pandemic brought it close to home, impacting them personally or through the people they loved most. No one escaped some impact on their mental wellbeing. That meant directing more energy to keep the psychological balance, ramping up self-care strategies, learning to understand what they were feeling, and tapping into their minds and emotions.

We have seen this increasingly discussed in the mainstream media, and social media is awash with daily self-care tips. There's

> Ensuring psychological wellbeing is part of a leader's role.

been no escaping that we're talking about, and working on, our mental wellbeing. We need this presence and openness to continue, to stick — not to revert to old behaviours after the acute pandemic phase.

Tokenistic efforts

One major mistake is taking a tokenistic approach to mental wellbeing. When I work with organisations on their mentally healthy workplaces strategies, we include recognition of annual days such as R U Okay and World Mental Health Week in their activity plans.

> One day of positive action doesn't absolve you from 364 days of inaction.

Why? Because awareness is the first stage of personal change. These days lift awareness, reduce the stigma and open conversations.

It is also about understanding that it's not necessarily about *your* mental health if this has never been a problem for you. Instead, it's learning to recognise when *others* may need help and providing the knowledge and language to safely ask someone if they are okay. If you saw someone clutching their arm, wouldn't you check on them?

But not everyone supports these campaigns in the workplace, and there are a couple of reasons for their resistance.

Firstly, one day of positive action doesn't absolve you from 364 days of inaction. It may appear tokenistic if you are not providing support for employee psychological wellbeing outside of these targeted days.

Secondly, the individuals we're asking to help lead or get involved in these events may have struggled (or be struggling), and no one has asked if they are okay or provided any support, so the activities appear superficial or ad-hoc.

Georgie agrees that events are a great starting point for organisations. But if that's the start and the end of their efforts, it's probably worse than doing nothing because it seems so disingenuous.

Workload

Early in 2021, I presented to a national audience on workplace mental wellbeing. While all attendees were there through a genuine desire to make their workplaces psychologically safer, a staggering 81% said that competing demands and conflicting priorities were barriers to working to reduce psychological harm risks in their workplace.

In the same week, I spoke with an experienced CEO, who asked me to help rationalise their workload. They were struggling with many discretionary change projects directed by the Board that did not align with the organisation's strategic vision or fulfil any mandatory compliance requirements.

Later that week, I had a similar conversation with a high-performing executive who doubted their ability to perform due to the disabling environment of work overload.

These are constant themes in my client work, regardless of sector, and they need addressing. I'll explore work overload further in Chapter Five.

Not a strategic priority

Who owns the portfolio of psychological harm prevention and all that entails in your workplace?

Does it sit with the OHS team or a member of the HR/OD team as an additional activity for when they have time?

The reality is that this work requires top-down involvement and active sponsorship — and appropriate resourcing. In Chapter Fourteen, we'll discuss your change team and provide more detail on the role of each tier in the organisation. For now, it's important to understand that this work requires strategic level oversight.

The proactive functions must be captured in a strategic action plan. Ideally, this is co-designed or (at the very least consulted) with a staff working group. The plan is reviewed and discussed in detail at executive and board levels. This is not a cursory glance and tick-off. If needed, make it a dedicated session so all parties fully understand the language, what the plan looks like in reality, the change facilitation required to drive and implement and embed this work, and the risks of not addressing these areas.

This work aligns with organisational development, workforce planning, attraction, recruitment and retention, human resource management, risk management, clinical risk management (health sector), occupational health and safety management, organisational strategy and operational management. It permeates every corner of your workplace, and the approach and resourcing must reflect this.

Do not risk paying lip service to this important work.

Work-related stress risks

There is a generally accepted list of workplace factors that if unaddressed, increase the risk of mental injury. These are:

- work demands too high or too low
- low levels of job control
- poor support (emotional, knowledge, tools)
- lack of role clarity (responsibilities, priorities)
- incivility
- poorly managed change
- bullying, harassment, discrimination
- occupational violence and aggression
- low recognition and reward
- poor organisational justice
- poor working conditions

- remote or isolated work
- violent or traumatic events.

Some industries naturally predispose workers to higher levels of risk. For example, our police and emergency services and health workers may be at heightened risk of exposure to violent or traumatic events. Health workers, first responders and even the education sector are at heightened risk of occupational violence and aggression. The impact of the pandemic has seen these risks spill over into hospitality and retail. These issues are very complex to address particularly as they concern client or customer behaviour.

However, there are several risk areas a workplace can focus on that relate directly to their accepted norms. I call these frequent flyer issues, and they cause significant impacts in workplaces and place employees at higher risk of mental injury.

The frequent flyers

These are the most common factors I see frequently in my work with clients and workplaces across various industries.

- unmanageable workload
- high demand/low control over work or events
- poor relationships (conflict, team dysfunction, poor leadership, incivility)
- exclusion
- bullying, harassment and discrimination

- workplace change (including poorly managed change and change fatigue)
- occupational violence and aggression.

All speak to unhealthy norms in the workplace. Each is unpacked in the following chapters — except for occupational violence and aggression (OVA).

A note about OVA

OVA is a complex and widespread issue that is prevalent across many industries I serve. I've spoken about OVA risk management systems and post-incident support systems at national and state conferences and implemented entire frameworks and change strategies in primary care and large public health services across my career.

The topic is too large and complex to cover in this book. Most high-risk settings have specific guidance material to support actions, including regulations and industrial frameworks. However, there are two fundamental gaps I wish to raise for your ongoing reflection.

- The post-incident follow up and support provided to staff (regardless of severity or frequency).
- The cumulative effect and very real mental health impact of even minor OVA events.

Given the frequent nature of OVA events (of all severities) in many workplaces, these events can become normalised. However, the impact on individuals must never be trivialised and should be assessed constantly with compassion and free of judgment.

It's personal

My daughter was held by the throat against a wall while being strangled by a patient on her ward. It was violent and traumatic, and while the personal duress alarm and her team response worked well, the ongoing impact of this event stayed with her for some time.

Months later, when her trauma started to surface and she shared this incident with me, I explored the post-incident support provided to her. Her response was, 'Mum, that happened ten times a day in there. I was asked if I was okay, and I just said yes. It was a normal event'.

I felt the impact of this event on multiple levels, so objectivity was a tad challenging. But I've interviewed numerous health professionals about the prevention and response systems and the reality of OVA on their work and their emotional wellbeing. I've conducted extensive research and discussed this at the systemic level exploring causation and internal and external contributing factors.

My conclusion remains the same. We must do more to support the emotional wellbeing of health and emergency service workers who face verbal and physical abuse and disgraceful behaviour from the people they are trying to help.

Look beyond the standard 'I'm okay' response.

In these workplaces, OVA events cannot be allowed to become normalised. The wellbeing of all workers — whatever the severity or frequency of exposure — must be monitored regularly, with genuine and sincere efforts undertaken to make sure they are travelling okay. And yes, that will take more time from the leader, but it's far less time than hiring and retraining.

Where serious events have occurred, this requires ongoing monitoring and check-ins. After the initial 'How are you travelling?' we have to look beyond the standard 'I'm okay' response. Particularly if they're surrounded by their peers when they're answering.

These discussions and support activities should be held privately, with no judgment or stigma and absolute compassion and support for valid feelings and responses to any type of violence and aggression.

While we do everything we can at system level to prevent OVA, everyone in the workplace can take steps to ensure appropriate support is provided to all staff exposed.

Chapter Summary

Terminology can be confusing. Look past it to what we are all trying to achieve — eliminating factors in the workplace that impact people psychologically.

Establishing psychological safety is not the same thing as mitigating psychological harm risks. There's a definite connection, but they are not opposites. We need to focus on both.

Mental injury rates are rapidly increasing, and regulators have developed new codes of practice to help workplaces address this.

Workplaces have always had duties under OHS legislation to protect employees from psychological harm; however, most proactive activity has centred around physical harm.

Many workplaces resist being proactive because of a head in the sand approach and stigma and myths about what it means to be a mentally healthy workplace.

Employees see through tokenistic efforts, so this approach can often be counterproductive.

Make this work a strategic priority.

Common factors contributing to psychological harm in modern workplaces need mitigating.

Take Action

Promote awareness of work-related stress risks across the organisation, starting with leadership layers.

Address common myths about what it means to be a mentally healthy workplace.

Start normalising messages about mental wellbeing in your workplace.

Reflect on the frequent flyer hazards in the following pages and hold safe and open discussions with teams about how they are travelling against these areas. Take special note of the presence (or lack) of psychological safety before asking these questions, or you're unlikely to get genuine feedback.

Add a *wellbeing check* into your 1:1 meeting templates. You can download a sample template from the resources section of my website www.tanyaheaneyvoogt.com/resources.

What Actions Will You Take?

1. _____

2. _____

3. _____

Chapter Five

Unmanageable Workload

One of the most common problems facing individuals at work is an unmanageable workload. Or, more precisely (from my perspective), the phenomenon of normalised work overload.

As the name suggests, this is where unmanageable workloads have become standard practice, an unwritten rule or general expectation. It can be more of a problem at leadership levels as many leaders feel they need to earn their stripes by putting in the long hours, but no one is immune.

It is a multi-faceted problem. Throughout this chapter, we'll examine contributing factors at individual, workplace, and broader environmental levels.

How does it happen?

There are forty hours in the working week (give or take, depending on your award or contract and your own choices and boundaries). Therefore it is basic mathematics that you can only reasonably be expected to manage forty hours of tasks, relationships and leadership duties in any given week. Less really if you consider time for amenity breaks.

Instead, people are being given increasing amounts of work to complete in those forty hours. Unreasonable amounts started as a little and, like kilo creep, are now a lot.

As you'll see in the model in figure 6, somewhere along the line, workplaces realise they can get an extra twenty per cent of discretionary effort out of employees when there's a pressing matter, crisis, or deadline.

It's not conscious — workplaces aren't usually that sinister. But most employees provide some level of extra effort and dig deep when they need to resolve a problem or meet a pressing deadline.

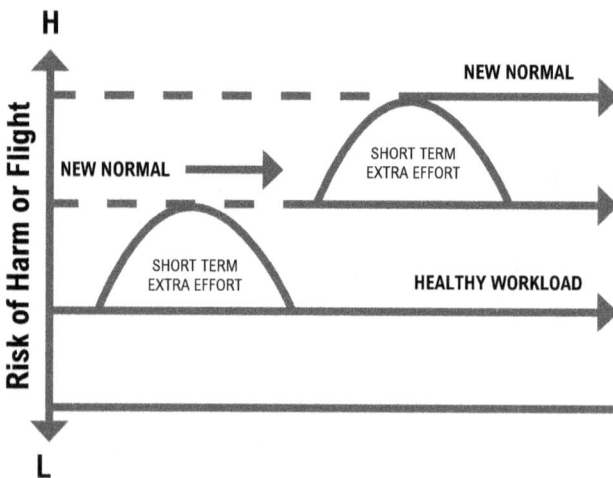

Figure 6: How normalised work overload develops

Yet what's happened is that this extra twenty per cent has somehow now become the baseline. This toxic cycle continues every time there's another pressing matter, crisis or deadline. And nobody challenges it.

Subconsciously we know employees can manage because we've seen them do it, so it becomes normalised behaviour.

The problem is that while these peak times can be managed in the short term, they are not sustainable. If left unmanaged, you place employees at higher risk of mental injury. From an organisational perspective, you risk regulatory action and losing (or breaking) your top talent.

In early 2021, I was asked to deliver a roadshow of leadership workshops to overworked and exhausted GP practice managers across regional Victoria. The sessions were about leading self and others and creating effective practice teams while understanding the common traps contributing to work overload and burnout.

> You risk regulatory action and losing (or breaking) your top talent.

The sessions were quite emotional. These leaders were clearly exhausted and grasping for ideas to get through another challenging year. There was a great deal of peer support, which was pleasing to see, and attendees relished the content with new ideas to explore.

I listened to a story from one leader who had worked ridiculous hours during the week and was then asked by her boss to come in on her weekend to set up a new service that they had no time, staff or energy to deliver. I asked, 'What would happen if you said no?' She looked shocked, and then realisation dawned. It had never occurred to her to say no. She was caught on the hamster wheel of work overload.

Many leaders who come to me for coaching have been caught in a similar way. They are desperate to find ways to manage what they feel is their inability to perform at the level required.

But it's not about their capabilities or performance. It's about unreasonable expectations.

Why don't people just say no?

It seems like a simple question, doesn't it?

Surely people can just say 'no' when asked to work extra hours or given too much work to manage in their allotted hours?

The problem is that people get caught on the hamster wheel without even realising it's happening, and this pattern of work overload becomes the norm.

Everyone else is working extra hours, so that's just the way things are around here.

There are other reasons too.

Fear-based environments

Chapter Three discussed the concept of psychological safety and the importance of creating environments where it is safe to speak up and where vulnerability is rewarded rather than punished.

In fear-based environments, you feel you can't refuse extra demands or say no. You genuinely fear repercussions or the lack of career progression if you speak up, push back or dare to renegotiate priorities.

Exploitative leadership

The boss doesn't want to hear how overloaded you are, do they? Because they're busy, and it's just the way it is around here, and they need you to deliver, so they can deliver, so the next layer up can deliver, and someone up the top will look good.

Sometimes this is as brutal as it sounds, while at other times, it's unintentional, and the boss is in as much of a pickle as you are, but neither of you knows how to break the cycle.

If you feel like you're in this space, start planning your exit.

Ourselves

The other contributing factor to normalised work overload is the inability of individuals to say no or negotiate better outcomes. This can arise for several reasons:

- lack of assertiveness
- poor boundaries
- people-pleasing tendencies.

These three areas are related.

Don't underestimate the importance of teaching staff assertiveness skills and maintaining boundaries to reduce the risk of normalised work overload.

Workplaces love people-pleasers, but be mindful of taking advantage of their continued willingness to take on extra work. You'll increase your risk of regulatory action or losing top talent.

Martyrdom

Two decades later, I still recall when, after going on about how busy and important I was at work and in our family, my brother's friend responded with, 'Do I smell martyr burning?'

Workplaces love people-pleasers.

I had no idea what he was talking about – literally or figuratively. I was far too busy being perfect to learn about worldly terms like that! However, with the benefit of hindsight, I realised I was riding high on my martyr's horse.

In the workplace, martyrs are those employees that work themselves silly because they believe (or like to tell you) that they are the only ones that can do that job or the only ones who will do it right.

Workplace martyrs believe the place will fall apart without them, and as a result, they struggle to take leave or even attempt to work reasonable work hours.

A word of warning

Be cautious when assigning labels to people. Rather than automatically formulating in your head the individuals who are people-pleasers, martyrs or passive communicators and making assumptions that there isn't a workload issue, take steps to examine the situation from multiple perspectives to get an accurate picture of the workload situation.

How do you know if someone really is busy?

How many times a day do you say (or hear) the phrase, 'I'm busy!'?

In 2021, I blogged, *Are you being deliciously well-utilised or distastefully overloaded?* I challenged people to question their use of the phrase 'I'm busy', proposing that when people say they're busy, they're not being specific and give no indication of the level of busyness.

For example, is it good busy or bad busy? Does busy keep you deliciously well-utilised? Or does it place you at risk of psychological harm?

I want to expand on this concept by including a new category. That of *demoralisingly under-utilised.*

You can see descriptors under each category and a rating scale in the following table. Use this in discussions with staff to help them be realistic about what 'busy' means.

As you explore the job demand and control model in the next chapter, you will understand the importance of ensuring staff are deliciously well-utilised. For now, ponder these descriptors and assess where you sit.

Demoralisingly under-utilised	Deliciously well-utilised	Distastefully overloaded
I'm bored, feeling unneeded or superfluous. I have no meaning or purpose in this role. I'm lacking sufficient mental stimulation. I'm not having my intellectual needs met. I don't see value in my contributions.	I'm perfectly utilised with great work challenges within my control. I have work tasks at the level that stretch, challenge and enable me to grow and achieve.	I have very high work demands with no ability to control the flow or regulate or negotiate priorities. I am working in a normalised pattern of work overload. I have not received support when I challenged my work demands or tried to negotiate more appropriate activity levels.
Passive or low strain	Active	High strain

Figure 7: Work utilisation model

You may find there are peak times where you move into *distastefully overloaded.* To avoid normalised work overload patterns, you must ensure you return to *deliciously well-utilised.*

How utilised are you currently in your role?

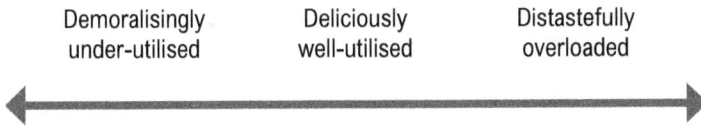

Demoralisingly under-utilised	Deliciously well-utilised	Distastefully overloaded

Imagine if you did something revolutionary, like asking your employees to rate where they are on this continuum? Or have leaders plot where they think each team member may sit?

What new insights would you gather?

And what steps could you take to ensure you maximise your individuals' wellbeing and productivity and address any patterns of normalised work overload?

Chapter Summary

An unmanageable workload is a common and high-risk issue facing modern workplaces.

Individual factors contribute to this issue, including people-pleasing tendencies, poor boundaries, lack of assertiveness skills and martyr traits.

Workplace factors increase the risk of unmanageable workload, including fear-based environments and exploitative leaders.

The word 'busy' is ambiguous, and leaders should have open and safe conversations with their team members to understand the actual level of work utilisation and address unsafe levels.

Taking Action

Teach leaders how to monitor their workload. Develop their assertiveness skills so they can negotiate their work volume and avoid having to flow it down the line to employees with less control over their roles.

Help individuals develop assertiveness and workload negotiation techniques. Arm them with responses such as 'I'd be happy to do this, however, given existing priorities and workload, I can't do it until next Wednesday. Would you like to look at my other priorities and see if we need to reassess those?'

Ensure leaders have regular 1:1 check-ins with their team members and discuss workload management openly and safely.

Resist the temptation to exploit well-meaning employees' discretionary efforts.

Establish a central project register that provides a high-level overview of divisional and organisational projects to ensure reasonable expectations.

What Actions Will You Take?

1. _____

2. _____

3. _____

Chapter Six

Job Demand and Control

In 1979, American sociologist Robert Karasek created the Job Demand Control model (figure 8), which assesses stress and stress factors in the work environment.

The model proposes that the higher the demand on an employee who has no, or low, control to regulate these demands, the higher the risk for psychological harm. In Chapter Five, we explored the concept of work overload, where an individual has high job demands. But it may surprise you to learn that employees with low job demands are also at risk of job strain.

This chapter looks at all four quadrants of Karasek's model and shows how job demands combined with job decision latitude (or control) can compound work-related stress risks.

The two axes in the model are job demands and job decision latitude. According to Karasek,[26] these demands could relate to:

- the volume of work
- timelines to complete the work

- the difficulty of the work, and

- the complexity of the work.

Job decision latitude reflects the combination of skills workers can use on the job and the worker's authority over decision making. It is generally grouped into the category of control.

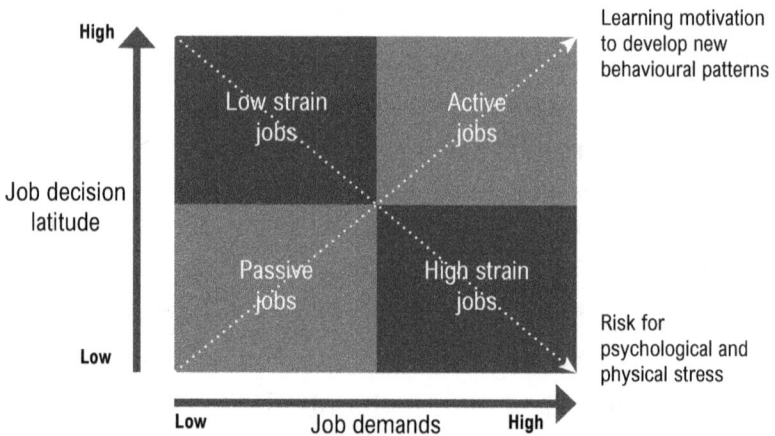

Figure 8: Job Demand Control model, Karasek, R. A. (1979)

High strain jobs

Consider the busy medical receptionists at a GP clinic or an Emergency Department. They generally have low (or no) control over their work and high demands. They essentially follow prescribed routines and work guidelines, yet they often face the brunt of angry and concerned patients and constantly deal with complaints.

This group has high demands (patient numbers, patient complaints, aggression) yet low control over their role, job design or environment.

When rolling out an Occupational Violence and Aggression prevention and management program in an acute regional health service in 2018, I undertook a series of staff consultations. One of many staff frustrations centred around a feeling of disempowerment because, despite the systems and structures in place to protect them, they couldn't really do anything to control the events.

High demand, low control

It is similar for customer service officers and employees down the line, inundated with work from leaders and unable or incapable of putting controls around the volume and timelines (for all the reasons covered earlier).

Low strain jobs

As the model shows, strain is also present in jobs with low demand, but the individual has high control or decision-making latitude. So, they're given autonomy over tasks but not enough challenge or meaningful work. Given work overload is one of the most pressing concerns in modern workplaces,

Many staff frustrations centre around a feeling of disempowerment.

how is it that people with not enough work are also at risk of psychological stress?

In his book, *Strive: Embracing the gift of struggle*,[27] Dr Adam Fraser explains that we need some form of struggle or goal to get out of bed in the morning. He says, 'the competitive advantage in business today is the ability to sit with discomfort and focus on the growth and development that comes from the struggle'.

In the workplace, the struggle may involve challenging tasks, stretch goals or learning and development. Fraser suggests that more than moving from our comfort zones into stretch zones, we need to move into stress zones, 'as long as we don't spend too much time there'. His research showed that it is devastating for humans when things are too easy. We need life to be challenging. He writes, 'We feel best about ourselves when we are being courageous and evolving while progressing towards a goal'.

Put bluntly, Fraser's book tells us that easy sucks. Our aim is for active jobs where individuals have challenges and struggles (within healthy stress ranges) and levels of autonomy and decision-making that are realistic for their role type.

Passive jobs

In 2018, NBC launched an American medical drama series, *New Amsterdam*,[28] based on the book *Twelve Patients: Life and Death at Bellevue Hospital* by Dr Eric Manheimer.[29]

In Episode 13 of Season One, the new medical director, Max Goodwin, is on a mission to identify staff with obsolete roles and redeploy them into meaningful occupations. He says he wants to find jobs that inspire people — jobs that make a difference. While making it clear that no one will be fired, he asks people to consider whether they are still being utilised in their roles or if they have become obsolete.

After one of his speeches, Max is advised about a guy in the basement who still prints X-Rays, so he heads down to explore. Sure enough, despite digital technology making his role largely redundant some ten years earlier, the fellow remains in his defunct department doing absolutely nothing.

Max asks the X-Ray tech if he likes his job. 'I used to. I loved it, actually. Everybody needed me.' Max says, 'I'd like to find you a new job. A job that makes you feel needed again. Would you be interested?' On this occasion, the fellow refuses, saying he'd rather just ride it out until retirement 'if you're not firing me' (probably the most realistic part of this episode).

In the meantime, people from all over the hospital inform Max that their roles are obsolete and no one would notice if they weren't there. They ask, excitedly, to be redeployed to roles that have meaning and where they can make a difference.

Max eventually presents his ideas for their future employment, and everyone is re-energised and excited by the opportunities. At the end of the scene, our X-Ray tech comes running into the meeting room, having decided to

Leaders can help people find meaning.

feel needed again and joining the others in a new meaningful occupation.

While this might seem far-fetched TV, the truth is that nobody wants to sit around feeling unnoticed, unappreciated, or insignificant.

Meaningful and enriching work

When it comes to psychological harm prevention and maximising employee mental wellbeing, finding meaningful and enriching opportunities and tasks is as important as reducing work overload risks.

Leaders can help people find meaning by demonstrating the link between job function and organisational outcomes. That doesn't mean everyone has to have an exciting job, but leaders can certainly help people feel there is meaning in even the most mundane role.

Actively look for ways to show meaning in roles that may not receive the same recognition and kudos as higher-profile roles.

Chapter Summary

Job demands and levels of control factor in work-related stress, compounding the risk of strain.

Low strain or passive jobs also impact individual mental wellbeing.

Workplaces should ensure all employees have meaningful and enriching work that is relevant to their position and capabilities.

Taking Action

Identify work roles in your organisation that have high demands and low control.

Monitor the wellbeing of people with high job demands and look at ways to control the risks associated at individual and organisational levels.

Help create meaning for people who have low job demands.

Consider Karasek's model in the design of jobs and identify opportunities for improvement to address potential impacts proactively rather than reactively.

What Actions Will You Take?

1. _____

2. _____

3. _____

Chapter Seven

Poor Workplace Relationships

WorkSafe Victoria describes poor workplace relationships as 'relationship breakdown with colleagues, supervisors or managers'. Basically, it's about conflict, which is an almost chronic problem. We'll look at some of the most common causes in this chapter.

I'm sure we've all experienced problematic workplace relationships. Do you remember what caused the tension or conflict?

Sometimes we don't even know how these things arise, we may just instantly not gel with someone, or something they say or do (or we think they said or did) can trigger us. The way they look or behave. It can be a values misalignment or a feeling that we aren't being treated with respect. Or sometimes we've just made a heap of assumptions about a person and their actions and motives.

Alexandra Rowe says, 'A lot of the matters we deal with relate to conflict, but when you dig a bit deeper, you find all of the other psychosocial hazards that are in there.' Because of this, workplace conflict can be complex and multi-faceted.

Ignoring the issue won't make it go away. While there's a powerful compulsion to put off taking proactive steps to address relationship tensions or conflict, these matters rarely go away with inaction. They continue to hold space in your heart, mind and gut.

Take a courageous step forward and face some of the positive actions outlined at the end of this section.

Common causes of workplace conflict

Many of these causes of conflict are interrelated. In figure 9 and the descriptors that follow, you will see some of the other frequent flyer hazards raising their heads.

Ignoring the issue won't make it go away.

At the end of the descriptors, there's a coaching tool to use on yourself, with your team or implement across the workplace to address relationship breakdowns, tension or conflict.

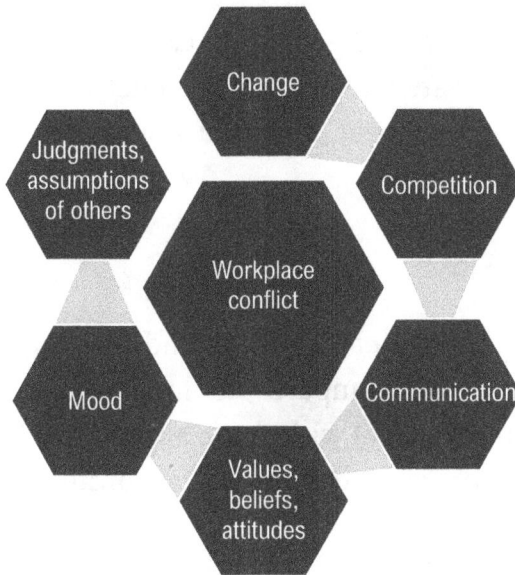

Figure 9: Causes of workplace conflict

Change

Change can be a catalyst for conflict for many reasons. Look out for these.

Scarcity mindset

People with this mindset tend to work on the premise that if 'you are to gain something, then I am to lose something'. We see this surface regularly during change, and it can be a common societal problem.

To get a clear idea of how the scarcity mindset works, think about the panic buying of toilet paper we saw across the country during COVID. People move into a mode where they think only of themselves and what they need, then claw over each other to get it. You can imagine how this can play out and create tensions and conflict when there is talk of targeted recruitment, reduced hours, or perhaps even closing business areas.

Comparative loss

People fear the impact of change and its comparative loss, which is when we compare our loss (perceived and not always based in reality) with those around us. When we feel unfairly treated, we act out or rebel accordingly.

Uncertainty and fear

Uncertainty breeds fear, which breeds unhealthy emotions. People don't regulate well and may be quicker to anger and not manage their communication as effectively as usual.

Fear is almost always present in any workplace change. Humans are conditioned to scan the environment for threats. We do so with even the softest murmur of change. It is why we must communicate early and transparently. But more on that later!

Competition

The most obvious cause of conflict here can be career ambition. We've all encountered that person who would throw their grandmother under a bus for career progression.

However, in today's resource-lean work-overloaded teams, it's more common to find people competing for a fair workload, different job tasks or opportunities and even time with the boss.

Across teams, we see competition for scarce resources — financial, physical or human resources. Conflict can arise if one group gets a larger share of the budget, additional staffing, or even capital infrastructure approvals and another doesn't. Competition for resources can fuel inter-departmental resentments; the 'us and them' divide that seeds and festers.

Communication

People communicate verbally, non-verbally and in written form. All three cause workplace conflict — as does the complete lack of communication. Passive-aggressive behaviours such as eye-rolling, head-shaking, and looking bored when someone is speaking can all create conflict. Emails sent without salutations or a perceived blunt message or directive are also significant triggers.

Personality styles, cultural differences, leadership capability, respect, civility.... The list goes on, and it's no surprise that communication is the topic of many a business book and training program.

Alexandra Rowe says communication issues

> Competition for resources can fuel interdepartmental resentments.

are a common problem in workplaces. Poor communication in times of change, lack of consultation with those impacted on the ground, and generally restricted access to leaders for everyday forms of communication, such as seeking clarity on roles and responsibilities or receiving feedback or support, are all major issues.

Incivility

Josie was a young new manager in her first managerial job since graduating. Her role involved liaising with top-level executives. She was initially afraid but then felt quite proud of doing so. Josie displayed great confidence and bonded well with the executive team, who responded well to her. All except one.

Josie was so distressed by this executive who would not return her 'Good morning' greeting in the hallway that she was convinced her job was in jeopardy. Over several months, Josie worked herself into quite a state, telling herself a story that this individual's lack of greeting meant he was unhappy with her, which would mean the CEO would dislike her, and her career would be at an end.

When Josie first raised this with me, she was highly emotional and anxious. She needed her income, and as she could not work out what she had done to upset this executive, Josie could only assume that she wasn't performing her duties adequately and was on the way out the door.

It took several coaching sessions to help Josie see this for what it was — incivility. And, sadly, poor leadership modelling.

I've lost count of the number of times I've had people or teams raise their concerns about how people communicate in the office. The two most common offenders are a lack of acknowledgment or greeting (saying hello, goodbye) and poor tone or lack of salutation in emails.

In September 2021, HRM Online magazine published an article by Dr David Hall on the eight negative micro-behaviours that HR should address.[30]

Number six on this list was the lack of greetings. Hall says that this can leave people feeling like they aren't important enough to be acknowledged. It is compounded when some co-workers are routinely greeted while others receive no response or if the individual who greets others unequally is a supervisor or manager.

Hall says that most managers receive some training on managing more major workplace issues such as bullying or sexual harassment. These seemingly less significant issues can be harder to respond to, but it's important to educate managers on the risks of not addressing them.

In 2018, Melbourne's Western Health trialled a new workplace civility program to address burnout. This was in response to a 2016 Victorian Auditor General's audit on the health sector's poor management of bullying and harassment.[31]

Michael Leiter, a global expert on workplace civility and job burnout, is involved in the Western Health civility program. He says, 'Saying good morning to a colleague can make the workplace a happier place, and can also make it a safer one'.

Leiter's research on Canadian health providers identified significant issues associated with incivility, including not saying good morning, excluding people, gossiping, undermining others, not showing appreciation, and general rudeness. The environment became toxic as incivility was reciprocated, and effort and motivation decreased.[32]

It's incredible that we need to remind people to do these basic things, but these simple practices of civility are fundamental to a sense of safety and inclusion.

Different values, beliefs and attitudes

Values, beliefs and attitudes primarily drive our behaviour in the workplace.

I recently spoke with a client who had two staff members at odds with each other. This senior executive had tried the usual interventions and was at a loss on the next steps. We unpacked things a little further to understand the source of tension. My client told me they both achieve their organisational objectives but have opposite ways of doing so.

One is all about task, discipline and getting stuff done. Her work ethic is no-nonsense, no chatting, just do it. The other is a warm and friendly type who loves interacting with others and enjoying her day. Both are performing, but this conflict is starting to affect the people around them.

My client explained that they are from different cultures and countries of origin. The cultural nuances of these two cultures could not be further apart (refer to Hofstede's

Cultural Dimensions below). While both achieve what they need to in the workday, neither appreciates how the other does it because it conflicts with their beliefs about behaving in the workplace.

This is one example of hundreds that could sit under this theme of conflict. Cultural, political, and social differences, as well as personalities, strengths and interests, can all clash as they relate to values, beliefs and attitudes.

We have seen this frequently over the past few years of COVID and earlier as social and political views seem to be increasingly polarised.

Hofstede's Cultural Dimensions

In the case of cultural differences, there are ways to develop an appreciation for each others' work styles. My client is progressing this, including having both individuals undertake a Strengths assessment to confirm that they add enormous value to their team while approaching their tasks from different perspectives.

The other resource I shared with my client is Hofstede's Cultural Dimensions.[33]

Dutch social psychologist and professor Geert Hofstede conducted one of the most in-depth studies of how values in the workplace are influenced by culture. He developed the six dimensions model, which maps cultures to help us better understand how individuals in teams and across the workplace connect and work together.

These six dimensions include power distance index, individualism, masculinity, uncertainty avoidance, long term orientation and indulgence.

It's a wonderful tool. If you have never explored this, follow the link in the references list.

Political and social beliefs

Working with people who hold vastly different values, beliefs and attitudes can be a bit of a melting pot.

Entrenched views can cause conflict and challenges.

There's rarely an issue discussed at the family dinner table or social barbecue that doesn't lead to some level of disagreement. Multi-generational families may experience this more acutely as the age gap widens. This is also reflected in the workplace, where a wide range of ages is represented. Entrenched views can cause conflict and challenges.

But while there will be people firmly gripping either end of the spectrum (see the model below), the majority are in what is sometimes referred to as the *movable middle*. They are open to others' thinking and hearing different ideas and opinions.

Majority

**Extreme
disagreement**

**Extreme
agreement**

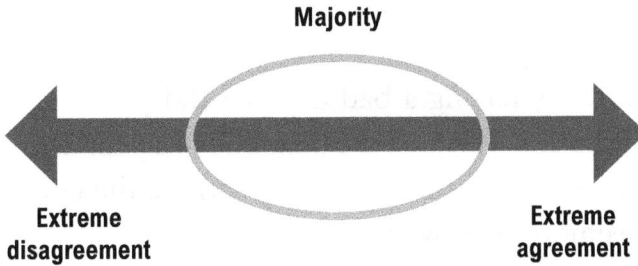

Figure 10: Values, attitudes and beliefs spectrum

Mitigation strategies

The following strategies can help bridge the gaps without people needing to agree completely.

- Make it safe for people to change their views. Our thinking can evolve, so share examples to enable people to do so without the fear of losing face.

- Set behavioural expectations and cultural codes.

- Get training on coaching people to unpack their values, beliefs and attitudes.

- Set expectations about respectful and constructive discussions.

- Teach people to approach discussions with a lens of curiosity, not judgment.

- Adhere to anti-discrimination legislation and set clear boundaries for ensuring an environment free from discrimination.

Mood

'Are you really having a bad day? Or did you catch it from your colleague?' This was the headline of a Human Resource Management Online article that described the contagion of negative emotions at work.[34]

Have you ever noticed how a negative or moody staff member impacts the entire workplace? This very real effect is called emotional contagion.

Leaders need to monitor their teams and address any pattern of negativity or mood that impacts others. This should include informal and more structured meetings to safely discuss any character changes in individuals. If the behaviour is out of character, the first instinct should be a wellbeing check, but if it is a pattern, address it promptly.

A note on mood: It is not uncommon to see worn-down, disaffected staff carrying around a rather dire mood. Take the path of compassion and tap into what has led them to this point.

Yes, you must do something, and you will likely coach them to take one path or another; but lead with compassion and curiosity rather than judgment. Genuinely invest in helping them address the issue.

Judgment and assumption of others

Have you ever made a judgment or assumption about a situation or a person that turned out to be completely wrong? It happens quite often in the workplace and can lead to conflict.

You may be familiar with the ladder of inference. Essentially it means that we make rash assumptions based on our perception of somebody — the way they look, their actions, their behaviours, and we mentally run up a ladder making all sorts of judgments about that individual.

For example, we see our colleague (with whom we secretly compete) talking to the boss. Instantly we're flying up the ladder and assuming the worst. 'They're getting preferential treatment!' 'They're reporting me for being late back from lunch!' 'They're trying to get the best projects!'

Rather than based on fact, we've made all these inferences from what we see. Then we believe these stories we've made up and act accordingly — when the truth is likely completely different.

Reframe negative emotions with positives.

In his book, *Positive Intelligence*, Shirzad Chamine explains that our mind can be our best friend or a powerful saboteur of happiness.[35] He writes that saboteurs are the voices in our heads that generate negative emotions in response to everyday challenges. Chamine's solution is to reframe the negative emotions with positives. In simple terms, if we negatively judge someone based on what we see, we can reframe that with a lens of compassion and empathy.

Chapter Summary

Poor workplace relationships can be linked to the common causes of workplace conflict.

Compounding multiple causes and other work-related stress risks contribute to personal tensions and reactions.

Relationship breakdowns can be complex and arise from deep-seated differences in values and beliefs.

Incivility is a common and troubling issue in workplaces, involving the absence of basic courtesies such as saying hello and goodbye or salutations in emails.

Taking Action

Embedding a culture code that is lived and breathed will help you hold people accountable for uncivil behaviours, poor moods and negativity. As leaders of change, help people (or yourself) find a more positive intent through emotions and hostility.

This quote from Joseph Joubert is a great guiding light. 'The aim of argument, or discussion, should not be victory, but progress.' Coach parties to find ways to make progress. Work with them and use the following reflective questions to get underneath the emotion of relationship conflicts.

Your goal is to help them understand the problem more practically and clarify what will happen if the conflict is not resolved.

Who is involved?

When does the conflict arise?

How do you feel when it happens? What is being triggered?

What do you believe is the 'source' of the conflict? (Refer to the common causes model in figure 9).

What other factors are at play? (e.g., power imbalance, workload, work culture, own fears, insecurities)

Considering the source of the conflict and other contributing factors, what are your options for progressing? Write down at least three constructive options, keeping in mind a win/win outcome.

On a scale of 1-10, how important is it for you to address or resolve this conflict?

How will you feel when you achieve that?

What can you do to maximise your chances of success?

What are your options if you are unable to resolve this conflict? Explore all options, including those you perceive as positive and negative. You can regain a sense of control over the situation by seeing that there are always choices.

What Actions Will You Take?

1. _____

2. _____

3. _____

Chapter Eight

The State of Exclusion

'I know of no rights of race that are superior to the rights of humanity.'
— Frederick Douglass, African American social reformer

In 2017, the Diversity Council of Australia and Suncorp partnered to develop a national survey to track the state of inclusion in Australian workplaces. Known as the Inclusion@ Work Index,[36] the survey is undertaken every two years and involves a nationally representative sample of three thousand Australian workers.

The results reveal that there are still many workplaces where exclusive or discriminatory behaviours are part of the norm. These behaviours are psychologically harmful and breach legislation. They prevail despite years of mandatory training.

The survey investigates two key questions:

1. How inclusive is the Australian workforce for a diversity of employees?

2. What impact does inclusion have on performance and wellbeing?

Results from the 2021 survey show more than a quarter of individuals completing the study had experienced or witnessed harassment and/or discrimination (exclusive behaviours) on at least one occasion in the previous year.

These rates increased significantly for certain diverse groups, with the highest experienced by Aboriginal and Torres Strait Islander people, half of whom report exclusion at work.

The five most discriminated groups were:

- Aboriginal and/or Torres Strait Islander people (50%)
- Religions other than Christian (48%)
- People with disability (45%)
- LGBTQI+ (45%), and
- Young workers aged under 30 (35%).

The survey findings reveal that everyday acts of exclusion are common in Australian workplaces and describe the situation as follows.

'Everyday exclusion tends to be subtle and common, including behaviours like not getting opportunities others receive, being treated as if you do not exist, being left out of work social gatherings, and having people make negative assumptions about your abilities based on your identity.'

Why inclusion?

The Diversity Council of Australia defines inclusion as 'when a diversity of people are respected, connected, progressing, and contributing to organisational success'.[37]

While the word is synonymous with diversity, inclusion is a basic human need. We all need a sense of belonging, to feel part of something and worthy.

The act of inclusion can be found at the heart of a mentally healthy workplace. Exclusive environments hamper learning, growth, and innovation because they are psychologically unsafe.

When we feel vulnerable, we are reluctant to offer new ideas or suggestions or admit to mistakes or gaps in knowledge for fear of being humiliated, shamed, embarrassed, or punished.

Inclusive environments tenaciously extinguish discriminatory actions, attitudes or behaviours. They actively invite contributions from everyone, model inclusive actions and promote healthy behaviours in others.

The Inclusion@Work Index 2021-2022 illustrates the positive impact of inclusion on employee engagement and workplace culture. Their studies show that workers in inclusive teams are:

Exclusive environments hamper learning, growth, and innovation.

- four times less likely to leave their job in the next twelve months
- ten times more likely to be very satisfied
- four times less likely to feel work has a negative or very negative impact on their mental health.
- five times less likely to experience discrimination and harassment
- eleven times more likely to be highly effective than those in non-inclusive teams
- ten times more likely to be innovative
- six times more likely to provide excellent customer service
- four times more likely to work extra hard.

Modelling inclusive actions involves challenging unhealthy behaviours in others. We all have a role to play in creating and sustaining mentally healthy workplaces that are safe and inclusive and enable everyone to thrive.

Support for organisational action

The survey results showed that three out of four Australian workers supported or strongly supported their organisation taking action to create a workplace that is diverse and inclusive.

How can you as an individual contribute to a more inclusive workplace?

What role can you play as part of a team to foster inclusion and extinguish exclusive or discriminatory behaviours?

And what role can you play in your workplace to influence change?

As Dr Martin Luther King said, 'In the end, we will remember not the words of our enemies, but the silence of our friends'.

Chapter Summary

Despite years of mandatory training activities, exclusive and discriminatory behaviours prevail.

Workers in inclusive teams are ten times more likely to be very satisfied at work, and eleven times more likely to be highly effective than those in exclusive teams.

Inclusive environments tenaciously extinguish discriminatory actions or behaviours.

Taking Action

Vigorously challenge discriminatory behaviours and actions.

Heavily promote the organisation's vision and values regarding diversity and inclusion.

Articulate the organisation's vision for a safe and inclusive workplace.

Actively involve the organisation in promoting days that foster inclusion.

Declare the organisation's values on inclusion and diversity in recruitment material and advertisements and set expectations for new incumbents before their appointment.

Be clear about the organisation's expectations around inclusion when onboarding and socialising new people.

Make leaders responsible for ensuring inclusive behaviours amongst their teams and the broader organisation.

Make leaders aware of the traits and expectations of safe and effective leaders.

What Actions Will You Take?

1. _____

2. _____

3. _____

Chapter Nine

Bullying and Discrimination

Workplace bullying

> 'Workplace bullying is repeated and unreasonable
> behaviour directed towards a worker or group of
> workers that creates a risk to health and safety. Bullying
> can take different forms, including psychological,
> physical or even indirect. It can be obvious, and it can
> be subtle, which means it's not always easy to spot.'
> — Safework Australia

Is your workplace creating an environment that is rife for bullying?

This chapter examines the reality and consequences of bullying and discrimination in the workplace. An industry case study and a self-assessment tool will enable you to determine your workplace bullying risk.

A large part of Georgie Chapman's work is investigating bullying allegations, which she describes as headline issues. The impact of COVID and external pressures over the past eighteen months means they are occurring even more frequently. 'People are more stressed and fatigued and not regulating as well as usual. And others are more sensitive because of the challenges and strain we're all experiencing. So it's a perfect storm, and we're seeing an increase in complaints as a result.'

Georgie says these are often formal bullying complaints that people want to have investigated or a psychological injury/work-related stress compensation claim. Claims are also made to the Fair Work Commission for a stop bullying order, but that's less frequent.

Aside from formal complaints, Georgie says the other workplace risk is staff turnover.

'Some people don't want to make a worker's compensation claim because it is still stigmatised to a certain degree. So they leave, and on their way out the door, they say, "Just by the by, this is one of the reasons that I'm leaving". Organisations might only start to realise there's an issue when several people have left. That's when they start to ask what's going on here?'

By then, Chapman says, the horse has bolted. Often workplaces then forget to address the root cause of the issue. Is it a leader in that particular chain? You've lost potentially some really good people and now have to engage in recruitment, on-boarding and retraining. And that can have significant costs for the organisation.

Failing to identify the problem

In 2016 the Victorian Auditor-General's report on Bullying and Harassment in the Health Sector[38] found that health sector agencies largely failed to identify bullying and harassment as a risk or manage it effectively.

The Auditor-General stated that while each audited agency described bullying as a 'risk to health and safety', none had applied standard risk management principles to the issue. That resulted in events being managed on a case-by-case basis with little focus on prevention or continuous improvement at an organisational level. This missing focus is all the more important, given that changing culture is a long-term challenge.

In other words, addressing bullying requires a proactive and transformational approach, not a reactive transactional one.

Is your workplace at risk?

Worksafe Victoria confirms that workplace bullying can happen in any workplace, and that under certain conditions, anyone could be capable of bullying-type behaviour.[39]

Environments that may be at higher risk of such behaviours have the following characteristics. Use the following table to self-assess and tick all those that apply to your workplace.

X or √	Characteristics that increase your risk of bullying behaviour
	High levels of unplanned, reactive and poorly managed change where fear and uncertainty are perpetuated.
	Autocratic or laissez-faire leadership styles. Autocratic styles are strict and direct, with command and control. Laissez-faire leaders rarely provide direction or clarity. They tend to leave subordinates with all the responsibility to solve issues.
	Lack of clearly defined roles and responsibilities or unclear communication channels.
	Unreasonable expectations regarding work volumes or timelines.
	Conflicts and disputes are left to fester and are not constructively resolved.
	High levels of interpersonal conflict.
	Unmanaged inappropriate and toxic behaviour.
	A lack of trust or confidence in management to resolve problems.

How does your organisation rate?

Discrimination

I asked Georgie Chapman about the discrimination element of the bullying cases she investigates, given the Diversity Council State of Exclusion index and other high profile data and work around equity, diversity and inclusion (including the Gender Equality Act 2020).

She says there can definitely be a crossover and that sometimes people will allege that the bullying has a discriminatory flavour. 'In a recent investigation, there was an allegation that the bullying was due to sexual orientation and gender. However, it can be difficult to substantiate what's in someone's mind unless it's explicitly verbalised.'

Chapman commented that prejudices remain in many workplaces and can be hard to pinpoint and address. It's not easy to support someone to unwind their attitudes, but it certainly must be part of regular educational programs and reinforcing behavioural expectations.

Policies and procedures are essential, as is an active investigation where particular issues are occurring — for example, only specific demographics are promoted.

While the new Gender Equality Act requirements have an impact, Chapman says the main problem is that there is still a lot of insidious discrimination that is not overt. It's much harder to distil and is a broader issue in our society.

Chapman says workplaces can minimise their risks by:

- monitoring appropriate workplace behaviours
- pro-actively looking at the hot spots
- genuinely monitoring the mental health of the workforce

- responding promptly and appropriately to complaints
- equipping leaders to identify the early warning signs of mental health problems, and
- making sure leaders are trained in reasonable management actions.

These proactive strategies are integral to avoiding losing good people and minimising the financial and reputational risks associated with a psychological injury claim.

Chapter Summary

Workplace bullying can be subtle, meaning it's not always easy to spot.

COVID has increased the prevalence of bullying behaviours in workplaces.

Aside from formal bullying complaints, organisations should remain alert to patterns in turnover and ensure exit interviews are always conducted to capture any problems.

Taking Action

Complete the bullying risk self-assessment tool. How did you score?

Create awareness of the higher risk behaviours present in your workplace.

List all the ways you proactively manage bullying and discrimination risks in your workplace.

What three actions will you take to create awareness of your bullying risks and improve how you proactively manage bullying and discrimination risks?

What Actions Will You Take?

1. _____

2. _____

3. _____

Chapter Ten

Mandatory Training Programs

One of the legislative requirements under Occupational Health and Safety (or Work Health and Safety, depending on your State) is that we proactively protect people from psychological harm in the workplace.

We do this by identifying practices known to increase the risk of work-related stress that can ultimately lead to psychological and/or physical harm and taking proactive steps to address or mitigate these risks.

In organisations of low maturity, most proactive activity tends to centre around an annual mandatory training program. There are limitations to this approach, so it's worth considering alternatives that will yield more sustainable change.

Mandatory training programs tend to be compliance-based, which means completion rates are the only measure of success.

We all know how this plays out in most workplaces. Managers are instructed to ensure all staff have their annual competencies completed by a specific date. They nag staff to 'just get it done' so their stats are up to date and the pressure from above is taken off.

I've been that manager.

And I've completed training feeling thoroughly bored and purely hitting 'Next, Next, Next' to get the thing done. It felt like an imposition rather than something beneficial, and I'd be lucky to remember anything if asked thirty minutes after completing the training.

Why?

Because in our current work overloaded workplaces, we approach training to *complete*, not to *learn*. We recall what we need to know to click 'Next', pass a quiz and print out our certificate. Then, it's largely forgotten.

We approach training to complete, not to learn.

This tick-and-flick approach to mandatory training is exacerbated tenfold if no other work is done on the other 364 days of the year. Forcing training on an entire workforce while ignoring poor behaviours outside of that results in widespread derision and disengagement.

Much like our own attitude to completing the task, organisations use these training programs to meet a legislative or regulatory compliance requirement, not to rectify cultural issues or truly effect individual change.

We need to be doing more. We need a proactive approach to preventing, mitigating and eradicating psychological harm.

Mandatory training and the state of exclusion

Certainly, the Exclusion@Work Index results showing discrimination is still rife in our workplaces despite years of mandatory training across the public sector beg the question: Is mandatory training working?

In 2016, Acting Auditor General Dr Peter Frost released his report on the audit *Bullying and Harassment in the Health Sector*.[40] Within the report, Dr Frost recommended mandatory training as a priority action to address the reported state of bullying and harassment in the health sector. However, he stipulated that 'agencies should develop and implement mandatory, comprehensive training and support mechanisms for managers on preventing and responding to inappropriate behaviour, bullying and harassment, including developing positive workplace cultures and relationships through good management practices'.

While this is clearly more than the typical tick-and-flick annual mandatory online training program, very few such comprehensive training and support programs exist in workplaces today.

Mandatory training is generally applied to meet OHS obligations and equal opportunity legislation. However, the evidence is clear that mandatory training (in its current form) on ethics, bullying and harassment, sexual harassment and diversity does little to change beliefs and attitudes. In fact, it can have the opposite effect.

In a March 2021 article in *The Conversation*,[41] Sue Williamson wrote that one-off sexual harassment training is ineffective and can make matters worse. Citing an American study, Williamson says 'researchers found men forced to undertake sexual harassment training become defensive, and resistant to learning.'

Other research highlights statistical significance in mandatory versus non-mandatory training, suggesting that voluntary participation will likely garner better results.[42]

> One-off sexual harassment training is ineffective and can make matters worse.

Pitch your training as strategically important rather than as a compliance requirement. This lends to a compelling case. There are great opportunities to improve the narrative around training programs by linking case studies and examples so people can emotionally connect to the purpose. Keep referring to strategic objectives where culture and people are first, with diversity strategies in progress.

Frank Dobbin and Alexandra Kalev wrote an article for *Harvard Business Review* titled, Why Diversity Programs Fail.[43] They observed that part of the problem is that companies are merely 'doubling down on the same approaches they've used since the 1960s, which often makes things worse, not better.'

Social scientists have proved that people often rebel against rules to assert their independence. As soon as training is mandatory and forced, resistance arises, and people will do the exact opposite of what they're asked. In change, this is referred to as *reactance*.

To illustrate this point further, let me share a rather bizarre story.

In his book *The Catalyst*,[44] Jonah Berger tells a story of when a warning became a recommendation. In early 2018, Procter and Gamble in the US had a small public relations problem when they relaunched a product called Tide Pods. These were powder pods wrapped in plastic — much as we often use now in our dishwashers. You simply popped one into the washing machine, the plastic outer dissolved, and the detergent cleaned your clothes.

The problem was that people were eating them.

An individual remarked (online) that the detergent pods looked good enough to eat, which set off an unfortunate chain reaction, and The Tide Pod Challenge went viral.

As you would expect, Proctor and Gamble issued subsequent advertising campaigns alerting people that you should only use Tide Pods for washing. Nothing else. And certainly not for eating.

What happened? Yep, even more people consumed them.

Telling people not to do something resulted in more people doing it. The warnings simply promoted the product further and subsequently became a recommendation.

I'm certainly not suggesting that employees would act this way and actively discriminate as a result of mandatory training.

But, as with most things, there'll be compliers, fence-sitters and downright resisters, and if these resisters *react* – they may sabotage your change efforts by doing precisely the opposite of what you ask.

Reduce the distance

One way we avoid reactance is to reduce the distance to change. This is essentially the gap between the current and desired states of individuals whose beliefs and attitudes we hope to influence.

I work to this (potentially controversial) strategy with my clients to implement Diversity, Equity and Inclusion activities.

Before we begin our communications and change activities campaign, we first need to understand the distance to change for the general workforce. Let's presume we want to move people's views on inclusion to ten (on a scale) when they are currently sitting at two. That's quite a distance.

If we bombard them with demands about what they should be doing and how they should be behaving at ten, we are likely to increase reactance and defiance. Nobody likes being told what to do, right? The change gap is also too wide, and they are unlikely to bridge it in a single step.

Instead, we focus on transitioning people along the scale. First efforts move people to a three perhaps, gradually reducing the distance to change and getting small wins along the way. We make incremental shifts that ultimately lead to bigger and more sustainable changes.

This is controversial because many people who have faced decades of marginalisation and discrimination are rightly tired of the gently-gently approach.

I completely understand and respect that. However, I'm yet to see a conversion of views in someone who is beaten over the head with the change stick.

I want to make lasting, sustainable changes in the workplaces I spend time with. If that means we need to go a little slower to achieve the desired outcome, then we'll do that.

What is the answer?

Frank Dobbin is a sociology professor at Harvard. His research has seen companies get better results when they ease up on the control tactics and introduce other strategies.[45] Dobbin recommends the following three factors as beneficial for addressing discriminatory beliefs and practices in the workplace.

- engage managers in solving the problem

- expose them to people from different groups (diverse groups to reduce bias), and

- encourage social accountability for change.

Don't throw out your training programs just yet!

This discussion is not intended to encourage widespread dismissal of mandatory training programs. They are, of course, an important first step under anti-discrimination legislation in educating staff on expectations around appropriate workplace behaviour.

What matters is that workplaces recognise mandatory training programs are not, in themselves, the answer.

The focus must be on transformative work rather than purely transactional as we know the tick-and-flick compliance-based approach has little impact on changing attitudes, values and beliefs.

Chapter Summary

In organisations of low maturity, there can be over-reliance on mandatory training programs to address issues such as bullying and harassment.

Develop comprehensive training and support mechanisms to help managers respond to inappropriate behaviour.

In your training activities, avoid reactance by reducing the distance to change.

Taking Action

Assess the effectiveness of your mandatory training programs. Are they the only activity throughout the year that reinforces behavioural expectations?

Expand your training programs to include skills development in responding to and addressing poor behaviours.

Engage your managers in solving the problem.

What Actions Will You Take?

1. _____

2. _____

3. _____

Part Three

Sustainable Change

Safe and
effective
leadership

PART THREE
PART THREE

Part Three
**Sustainable
Change**

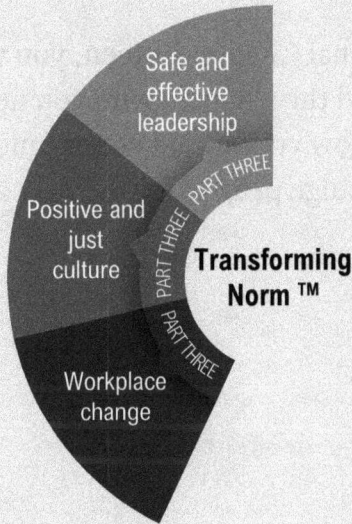

Positive and
just
culture

**Transforming
Norm ™**

PART THREE

PART THREE

Workplace
change

In Part Three, we look at the final segments
of the Wheel of Change.

Chapter Eleven: Workplace Change

Chapter Twelve: Positive and Just Culture

Chapter Thirteen: Safe and Effective Leadership

In the final Chapter Fifteen, you will discover how
to Lead the Change, who you need in your team
and how you should communicate and initiate
your change project for the best chance of success.

Chapter Eleven

Workplace Change

Poorly managed change is a major contributor to work-related stress.

Even though change is a constant, there is little support for workers to transition through a change process. Most leaders charged with driving change have received no formal training in change management methodologies. The result is environments that *tell* people what is happening and expect them to comply willingly.

This chapter explores change management as a discipline and considers how it differs from project management. We look at why poorly managed change has such an impact on individuals in the workplace. You can take

> Organisations don't change, people do.

simple steps to lead change in a way that will enhance your culture and your people's psychological wellbeing, rather than detract from it.

Good change management is about understanding that *organisations* don't change, *people* do. And the carrot approach is far more conducive to a safe and happy workplace than the stick.

Poor organisational change management occurs in workplaces where there is:

- not enough awareness or willingness to consider the potential impacts of change

- not enough consultation or communication with those impacted, recognising that not all individuals are affected in the same way during any change activity. (Note that merely fulfilling the EBA change impact steps does not cut the mustard here.)

- not enough practical support for employees during the transition, or

- a practice of using 'change' to circumvent due process.

So, what exactly is change? It is a process of transitioning from a current state to a future state.

And change management?

Change management is a formal discipline where we transition the people through organisational change.

It differs from a linear project approach which tends to be more autocratic, directed and task-focused, checking off milestones on the plan and telling people what will be happening. People are rarely informed about why the change is happening and why it matters to the organisation. They are merely told to jump from one state to another without explanation, understanding or support. When all the project steps have been completed, the change project is considered a success.

But if the people have not transitioned, if they're not working in the new way, then nothing has progressed.

One of my executive coaching clients shared a fitting example. Some six years ago, their workplace implemented a new clinical pathway. This different way of managing a particular client group required a considerable change of practice for the clinicians involved.

On paper, the project was completed and deemed a resounding success. The new clinical pathway was defined and pushed out to clinicians who were told this was how they were to do things from then on.

> Telling people what will happen is not change management.

Six years later, my client tells me that less than twenty per cent of the clinicians are using the pathway.

This is a classic project approach. Telling people what will happen is not change management. Organisations with a 'tell' approach tend to neglect aspects of change that can enhance culture and wellbeing.

Why does change create stress?

Workplace change has enormous potential for stress because we fear loss far more than we value gain. Fear creates anxiety and all manner of resistant behaviours.

When faced with workplace change, most people check internally for threats. What will this mean for me? What do I stand to lose in this change? Rarely are our first thoughts 'Oh, this will be a great opportunity!' or 'Wow, what a great move for the business!' And those tasked with having to lead, implement, or sell a change initiative usually respond with something like, 'How the hell am I going to do that on top of my current workload?'

Change creates stress because of uncertainty about how it will impact those who need to make a transition and those responsible for implementing the change work.

Despite change being a constant in our world, few workplaces train staff on how to lead or manage through change. By adopting a formal change management approach, workplaces will eradicate the factors we see in poor organisational change.

Backed by decades of global research by Prosci, applying a change management approach means you are:

- six times more likely to achieve or succeed in your change objectives

- five times more likely to complete your project on or ahead of schedule, and

- thirty per cent more likely to be on or below budget.[46]

But more than that, you will achieve your change with a workforce that feels valued and supported and significantly reduce your risk of losing good staff.

Human beings need choices

By consulting and communicating effectively in line with change management principles, employees will have chosen to transition to the future state rather than just being told to get there.

Think about the last time someone told you to 'just do' something. If you've ever raised teenagers, you'll understand this approach rarely (if ever) works. We tend to *react* and *resist* — even if we agree!

To avoid this state of reactance, clever change and transformation practitioners frame change messaging in a way that enables people to choose to transition independently.

Most of the time, we do this by providing compelling reasons for the change. We clearly answer:

- Why is this change happening? (What's driving the need, externally and internally.)
- Why is it important to the organisation?
- What are the business reasons for the change?

- What will happen if we don't make this change?

The important step here is framing messages to engage those impacted by the change. That's the 'What's in it for me' or WIIFM message.

Insisting on change because of new legislation or 'just because' does not engage hearts and minds. Sometimes you need to gild the lily and carefully craft your 'why' messages. Perhaps you'll need to subtly talk about what will happen if the organisation doesn't make the change — not as a threat or inducing more anxiety, but supportively to help people open their minds.

When I support my clients in doing this, we strategically identify pain points in the business. If we need to engage a particular group or an entire layer, we explore the pain points for that group and look at how we can link the 'why' of the change to address these. That gives them a compelling reason to buy into the change.

One recent example is engaging people in the Gender Equality Act requirements. Yes, there's a moral argument, but it's a tough sell for overworked leaders who struggle to manage their workload because they can't recruit to their departments.

A far more compelling case for engaging in internal activities to boost gender and intersectional inclusion may be the organisation's ability to attract more candidates and access a wider candidate pool to recruit from.

Give people a menu

In *The Catalyst*, Jonah Berger talks about giving people a menu to enable them to make choices and ease the impact. Choices mean they have some control, which we all desperately look for during change.

During a change project, we can cleverly design choices that still align with our change goals and help us keep moving forward. You could provide a menu of choices or explain the end goal and let people know they have control over how to get there.

There are many ways to help people feel more in control, increase their engagement and reduce their resistance to the initiative.

Intent and integrity are essential here. If you misapply this tactic, it will be hard to win the people back. So if you plan on adding 'be exited from the organisation' as a choice for people, perhaps think again.

During COVID, I provided suggestions to my newsletter subscribers on how they could support their teams to feel they had some control, given so much rapid change and many people's sense that life was completely out of hand.

While leaders grappled with managing flexibility requests and virtual working during lockdowns and homeschooling while keeping their department functioning, I made the following suggestions for their teams. These gave some control to the uncontrollable and offered choices while clearly communicating expectations.

People were *asked* rather than *told,* but the leader set the parameters, so they also got what they needed. They asked:

How would you like to navigate lockdown?

- work flexibly
- stay with my current hours
- take leave.

How would you like to hold our 1:1 touch base meetings and check-ins?

- between 8 am and 12 noon
- between 1 pm and 5 pm
- before work hours
- after work hours
- via Zoom
- via phone.

What treat do you prefer for our virtual team meetings?

- A morning tea care package delivered at meeting time.
- An e-voucher for you to use at a time that suits you, perhaps with your family.

So instead of groaning about (or looking for an excuse not to attend) another virtual team meeting, they're excited about making a choice.

Think about how you can frame your required changes as a menu.

Barriers to engaging employees in change

One of the main challenges when trying to engage employees in organisational change initiatives is that change may have been managed poorly in the past.

Every workplace has a history. And often, what we see in organisations with no awareness of change management principles is a classic 'tell' approach to change.

Organisations should also avoid using change to circumvent due process. It's hard to recover from major restructures or realignments undertaken to intentionally avoid performance conversations, performance improvement processes or the hard yards of exiting an individual from the organisation.

Anyone who has led a performance improvement process will tell you it is time-consuming and mentally demanding. It also takes a particular skill-set — not least perseverance, emotional regulation and the ability to follow a robust structured process. Many leaders lack the skill or will to do this, so sweeping changes are made to avoid due process.

Believing this will save you time is a falsehood.

Rather than address one bad apple, you impact many, and even a whole organisation, to avoid one difficult moment or time-intense period. Ultimately you lose the respect of your people and create an environment of distrust and fear, giving change a bad rap in the process. These are common examples. One speaks to an old fashioned leadership approach, more dictatorial than collaborative, and the other to poor organisational justice.

How can you overcome a poor history of change?

If you're trying to move forward more constructively and want to show your people you will be doing 'change differently' from now on, the best thing you can do is own this organisational error and consign it to history.

Help people draw a line in the sand.

Be open and honest. Admit you have not always managed change well in the past, and be explicit about how you will do things differently.

Clearly articulate:

- What will change about how you do change?
- How will you be leading change from now on?
- What opportunities will staff have for co-design, collaboration and input?

A successful example

One of my change coaching clients, Rachael, spoke about how successful this approach had been. As a senior executive, she was driving complex service-wide change across a workplace with a poor history of change and significant cultural issues. We discussed the organisational history and how to take steps to recover from this before moving too far into the new change work.

Rachael's change approach started well before the implementation activities by bringing together a large staff group and demonstrating how this change would be different. More open. More transparent. More collaborative and consultative. (Remember that project work is task-based and linear, while change work is about people's hearts and minds.)

After two meetings, the feedback was phenomenal. Rachael said there was excitement, optimism and hope in the room. Something that was rarely seen before. In speaking with the group, she called out the poor history, declared the intent to do things better and identified the primary role the group would play in designing and supporting the change.

She said staff had spoken openly in the meeting, saying how thankful they were to hear that message and agreeing that change hadn't been done well before. They were grateful for the new approach and excited about their involvement.

It takes true leadership to acknowledge past mistakes. But the trust and respect you'll earn in the process are well worth it.

Why people resist change

In any change initiative, practitioners anticipate and plan for resistance. It can come in many forms, from all levels of the organisation (including management), and for many different reasons.

In general, you'll find the basis for resistance within the following arguments.

- They disagree there is a need to change. They don't believe there is anything wrong with the current state.

- They agree on the need to change but don't believe the proposed solution is the right one.

- They resist the sender of the message. They don't like the messenger or feel they are not the appropriate person to be presenting the change.

- They resist because they are uncertain of the implications and unclear about what's in it for them.

- They fear loss. Loss of role, hours, title, status, job task, face, control, and loss of productivity if additional work is required. Loss can take many forms over and above financial, so consider all aspects that may arise from the change you wish to implement. Note that this does not have to be an *actual* loss; it is the fear of loss that fuels resistant behaviours. In good change management practice, we avoid this by providing appropriate and clear information early on.

- They resist because they can, and it's fun, and they're jaded.

- They were told, not consulted (a common reason for resistance).

- They are saturated in changes or work overloaded (exacerbating the work-related stress risks).

Many factors at play in the workplace and personal circumstances influence employees' response to change initiatives. (Refer to the factors of influence in Chapter One). Any previous history of change also has huge implications for how people embrace or resist change in the workplace.

It's also important to note that not everyone is impacted equally by any change.

All of these explain why a change management approach works better than telling. The people side of change needs to be considered to reduce the risk of psychological harm and build a positive and safe culture, not a fear-based one.

A point of clarity

Many of my learned consultant colleagues claim that the concept of people resisting change is rubbish. They cite human evolution and our constant adaptability as proof of this falsehood. I want to highlight the subtle distinction they are making, as I often talk about change resistance as a significant issue in the workplace.

Do human beings resist change?

No. As a species, we embrace change. Obviously. We have evolved. We are adaptable. We are flexible. So on the human or evolutionary level, perhaps people don't resist change as an overall concept.

We resist the uncertainty that change brings.

But in the workplace, they resist because of how change is administered and the uncertainty and fear of loss that so often accompanies it. This fear leads to a fight or flight response, and the fight manifests as resistance.

They may not resist the actual change itself (this is important), but they do resist the *uncertainty* that change brings.

What do you think? Have you seen people resist change in the workplace?

What about you? Have you resisted (inwardly or outwardly)? What was the cause of your resistance?

Change saturation leads to change fatigue

According to Prosci, 'change saturation occurs when the number of changes you're implementing exceeds the capacity of individuals in your organization to effectively adopt and use those changes'.[47]

Your change initiative can only be deemed a success if the people on the ground are working in the new way, months after the project has formally ended. At that stage, they have adopted and are using those changes.

Change saturation poses a risk to the success of your initiative and can lead to disengaged and frustrated employees who are feeling the effects of too much change. This is change fatigue, which can present as active resistance, dysregulated behaviours (frustration, emotion, anger) and even full-blown job dissatisfaction.

We risk churn here, losing good people who feel impacted by their inability to give their all to competing projects. It is particularly true of our high performers.

So what can you do?

Senior leaders of change often feel helpless and unable to control the pace due to external demands and compliance requirements. You know more changes will impact your people, but you have no choice given the demands imposed upon you and your workplace.

But there are ways to minimise change saturation and change fatigue for yourself and your people.

It's easy to get caught up in the hamster wheel, so your first step in managing overwhelm is to list the initiatives that are planned or currently underway in your organisation.

Separate these into *must have* and *nice to have* projects. What's the difference?

'Must have' changes are generally in response to external demands or risks – such as COVID responses, direct risks or threats and regulatory requirements.

'Nice to have' changes are usually driven by internal demands and could include new service development, new technology, or quality improvement activities.

Look at your lists through a strategic lens. Ensure that each change directly correlates to your organisation's direction and vision. Cut those that don't. Now apply a resourcing lens to your projects and defer or cut any you can't effectively support.

Ask the hard questions

You may need to ask some hard questions when looking at your lists.

Why are we really doing this?

Why are we doing this now?

Why is this the priority?

What would happen if we park or cut this?

You may have to sacrifice some 'nice to haves' to ensure you can successfully transition your people through the 'must have' projects. But your change success and people's ability to transition through it will be strengthened.

A word of warning: workplace culture, psychological harm prevention, and building psychological safety are 'must have' projects.

Little changes can equal big headaches

Have you ever made a slight change that created a big headache? You know the kind. Moved someone's desk around? Swapped chairs? Tweaked a roster?

Even seemingly helpful small changes can cause big dramas for some people, especially if they aren't aware of the reason for the change or given options.

In one particular coaching session, a client was coming out of a particularly tricky period that arose from a seemingly trivial change.

He'd processed the change he wanted to make and thought about the impacted parties. He's a good soul who is very mindful of his employees' needs, so this was done with absolute positive intent. But, like most busy leaders, he was keen to move to the future state vision and get the task done. So he pushed forward and told people what was happening.

Two months of chaos ensued with emotional outbursts and regular threats of resignations that took a lot of effort to settle

We all like to be involved, consulted and given a choice.

down. 'It was such a small change, and staff stood to benefit,' he said. 'I just couldn't believe what all the fuss was about.'

It seems fair enough, doesn't it? But there are some cautionary tales here.

You need to remember that little changes can still have a big impact.

Just because we don't see an issue doesn't mean it doesn't exist.

We all like to be involved, consulted and given a choice.

For leaders, moving a desk or making a quick change to a schedule may seem totally insignificant. Particularly given some of the complex challenges and issues we deal with.

But if we aren't the ones impacted by the change, can we really make that call?

Have you experienced a big drama from a little change?

What might you do differently if you had your time again?

Chapter Summary

Poorly managed change in the workplace is a common cause of work-related stress.

Adopting a change management approach will minimise work-related stress risks and maximise your chances of change success.

Don't underestimate the potential of little changes to have a big impact.

Frame change messages in a way that engages the hearts and minds of the people impacted by the change. Don't just tell people.

Plan for resistance by understanding why people may resist your change and putting prevention plans or strategies in place.

Avoid change saturation and fatigue by clearly separating 'must have' and 'nice to have' projects and tying them to the organisation's strategic objectives.

Organisations with a poor history of change can reset by drawing a line in the sand, calling out their previous flawed approach and clearly stating how future change will be done differently.

Taking Action

Create a change register of 'must have' and 'nice to have' projects.

Build in a series of questions that rationalise and prioritise projects.

Create awareness of change saturation and fatigue.

Clarify the difference between project management and change management.

Train leaders in the basic principles of change management.

Highlight the risks of multiple major change projects.

Create awareness of why poorly managed change is a work-related stress factor.

Commit to 'doing change differently' in your workplace.

What Actions Will You Take?

1. _____

2. _____

3. _____

Chapter Twelve

A Positive and Just Culture

'A pattern of thought or behaviour in a person is a habit.
A pattern of thought or behaviour on a team is a norm.
A collection of norms in an organisation is a culture.'
— Dr Timothy R Clark

Culture is often defined as 'the way we do things around here'.[48] It is the unwritten and unspoken rules and norms of the work environment and can exist as a vibe, a feeling or a mood.

This chapter considers what it takes to establish and maintain a positive culture, how to lead culture change, and how just one lone nut can start a movement.

Why is culture so variable?

Given that culture is set and adjusted by humans, it is often variable across workgroups, and many sub-cultures can exist rather than one dominant culture.

If the sub-culture behaviours align with a positive dominant culture, they do not cause problems. But if sub-cultures are toxic, they need addressing before they spoil the dominant culture.

We can also draw on positive sub-cultures if the dominant culture needs remediation to help influence positive change.

When leading the change to a mentally healthy workplace, we aim for a positive and just culture. This is where:

- Organisational justice is strong, meaning fairness and transparency of actions.

- Leaders actively model the behaviours congruent with a mentally healthy workplace.

- Behavioural expectations are clear for all to see, upheld and protected.

Culture enables outcomes

Too often, culture is seen as something we do if we have time, rather than the enabler of organisational outcomes. I often wonder why organisations don't place as much focus on people and culture as they do on their financial assets.

In the public sector, there is a requirement to develop asset management plans as part of the Asset Management Accountability Framework (AMAF).[49] It's a duty under the Financial Management Act. This framework requires identifying critical assets and detailed reporting of how that asset is maintained and nurtured, recognising its value in the organisation.

Ideal operating conditions are established, monitoring regimes and maintenance schedules are created, and due attention is paid to that piece of machinery, pool car or expensive piece of technical equipment.

So why don't organisations do the same for our most valuable assets — people?

Why don't we recognise that people, not machines, are enablers of our organisational outcomes and success?

Some organisations do this so well, as you will read below. However, many CEOs still see culture as something to worry about if they have time. Or perhaps, in AMAF language, only if there's a major breakdown.

Culture's not yoghurt, so don't set and forget

A workplace culture evolves constantly. Each leadership shift, every exit and entry, new or changed work team or new project team has the potential to modify culture.

There is a tendency in culture change activities (much like general project activities) to imagine the efforts have a set

> Many changes fail because we take our foot off the accelerator too soon.

timeline and clear start and finish dates. But that is where things go wrong.

In his book, *Leading Change,* John P. Kotter says many changes fail because we take our foot off the accelerator too soon.[50] We can't ever do this in maintaining a positive and just culture. It is too vital to neglect and requires constant focus and vigilance.

So rather than having a culture change *project,* have a positive and just culture *philosophy.*

A culture first philosophy

Leisure Networks[51] has a culture first philosophy. It is a community-focused organisation based in Geelong that provides disability services, support for active living and support for community sporting clubs across the region. For three decades, Leisure Networks has pursued a vision of capable, healthy people and inclusive communities.

Pip Jankowski, Executive Director of People Culture and Capability, describes their approach to culture as a relentless focus. They are ferocious in guarding their positive and just culture.

Long before a new incumbent hits the ground, they are socialised into the organisation's norms. Job advertisements talk about the culture before the job description. Culture is modelled as a key attribute, providing an attractive employee value proposition.

This ensures that behavioural expectations are clear, that only people with aligned values are attracted to the workplace in the first place, and that the relentless focus is regularly communicated for all to see.

Leisure Networks talk about their culture front and centre on their website, with their values and purpose stating that their culture 'is a living thing and it changes and adapts as our organisation grows.' Culture is spoken about at every opportunity. It is a dynamic workplace function rather than something that sits passively in the background.

It takes just one lone nut

In his popular TED talk, Derek Sivers says that it only takes 'one lone nut to start a movement'.[52] Like many of you, I have been that lone nut.

I remember sitting in a Beyond Blue workshop unpacking the Mentally Healthy Workplaces framework and implementation guidance. The clear message was that any culture change work required absolute commitment and support from the executive. I didn't have that in my workplace at the time.

Now, I know the theory that true change needs to be led from the top. I also know that many of you will be leading change from within, not from the top.

If changemakers gave up easily, where would we be right now?

There is no doubt that things are easier if the executive sponsor (and model) culture change; we aim for that in every change initiative. But my point is, we don't give up if they aren't. I speak with many people who are passionate about creating mentally healthy workplaces and have poor or no leadership support.

If we don't give people the ability to influence change around them, we risk disengaging those who have a burning passion for improving things. And I simply cannot accept that. The world desperately needs those lone nuts. The case for change is clear.

If you need to, be that lone nut.

So, if you need to, be that lone nut. Here are some thoughts on how to influence those in your immediate circle and draw on other champions to lead the change.

Use sub-cultures and culture champions

If you don't have the luxury of genuine and visible sponsorship from the top, mobilise your culture champions and create positive sub-cultures.

This has an amazing impact on the people within those teams or workgroups. It starts a groundswell, and soon the engagement survey results will speak for themselves. Others will get a healthy dose of FOMO and catch on.

Leaders will soon realise they're losing people to your team, attracted to the new culture you've established. Their people will hear from your team about how things are done over here, and they too will want to be part of that action.

By focusing on your inner circle, those areas you can control and influence, you can still make positive change for those around you — if not for the entire organisation. The only limitation is that this approach is person dependent.

We don't change the systems or behavioural expectations for the organisation. We don't write new organisational norms, and if our culture change champions exit, we are back to square one.

In a workplace where culture is poorly valued, the sub-cultures will always be leading change and creating pockets of positivity and effectiveness, rather than truly sustainable enterprise-wide transformation.

This can be disheartening, but sometimes the changes stick. And maybe, just maybe, as a lone nut, a little of your legacy will remain.

Fixing a toxic culture

Take a deep breath; this is going to take courage and persistence. But oh, how rewarding! Gather your change team around you (external supports if you don't have internal supports) and carefully map out your change plans.

As a rule of thumb, follow these steps:

1. Design your future state vision for the culture

What does your new culture look like (or need to look like) to support your organisational outcomes?

What does it mean in terms of attitudes and behaviours within the organisation?

Ideally, you will have co-created the future vision with groups or all employees to ensure buy-in and engagement. (See the case study at the end of this chapter for an example of how to do this.) You must be very clear on what your future state of culture looks like and why.

2. Draw a line in the sand and communicate the new behavioural expectations

Communicate acceptable and unacceptable behaviours in ways that are meaningful and understandable. Give clear examples, not ambiguous statements such as 'Be respectful.'

Make sure you can answer the following questions confidently and clearly.

- What do the new expected behaviours look like?
- How will people be supported to learn and model the new behaviours? (see Point 3)
- When is everyone expected to hold to these new behaviours?
- What won't be tolerated any longer?
- Why is this change necessary?

- Why will this change be different to previous (failed) attempts?

3. Give people the knowledge, support and training to make the required changes

This may involve:

- change coaching to support leaders responsible for the transformation program
- coaching to increase self-awareness and challenge unhelpful values, beliefs and attitudes
- training activities that foster inclusion and an appreciation of individual differences and the value of what each individual brings to the team.

The most critical activity supporting change is when leadership models the new values, behaviours and interactions. If leaders are not walking the talk, no amount of selling will help you.

4. Actively address poor performance with individuals directly

Unfortunately, the problem will not go away on its own, so you'll have to bite the bullet and go down the path of performance discussions and improvement plans if that's what your industrial instruments instruct.

Many negative cultures comprise disaffected staff who grew tired of leaders tolerating poor behaviours. So much so that they gave up and decided to become difficult as well.

We must hold the line on poor behaviours. This becomes even more important when we announce and commit to a culture change.

5. Exit staff who are not aligned

Whether it is about skill or will, some people will need to exit as you move towards your new future culture vision.

One of the most common things we see when tightening cultural boundaries is some flapping of the wings. People test the limits, and, in some cases, they act out and become even more difficult.

I have seen this often in teams where the culture was so bad they were considered psychologically harmful. When new behavioural expectations are set, we clip the wings of difficult people. They make a lot of noise, but we must hold the line.

They have a choice. They can either agree to conform to the new expectations or leave. If the toxic behaviour (and their power) has been going on for a long time, they will generally exit.

Either outcome is good. The important thing is to hold the boundaries firm when they are challenged. Hold the line despite the temptation and no matter how hard it becomes.

It is essential to support leaders who are transforming difficult teams during this transition phase. It's tough work, draining and packed with self-doubt. Make sure there is appropriate support, including industrial relations and legal backing.

6. Then recruit and socialise into the new culture

When you are moving in the right direction, recruit to the future vision. Do not make the mistake of bringing great people into the workplace too early.

The exceptions may be where that person will be part of a sub-culture that is already working in the future state way, and they will be supported and informed that broader cultural change is progressing.

Stop throwing Mother Teresa into the gladiator's pit

It is tempting to fix a toxic culture by recruiting new blood. In other words, we feel that socialising new people into the organisation who model the values and behaviours we want to see will solve the problems, and everything will be peachy.

Unfortunately not.

Recruiting great new people into a workplace with a poor culture without taking steps to address the poor behaviours is akin to throwing Mother Teresa into the gladiator's pit.

This is potentially psychologically harmful for the new incumbent and will likely result in one of three outcomes:

1. The person is indoctrinated into the poor behaviours purely to survive.

2. Their wellbeing is impacted as they attempt to socialise into a harmful culture.

3. They exit the organisation and take your reputation with it, making future hires even harder.

Socialising new people into the future state culture is indeed a transformation strategy, however there are steps you must take first.

Case study: Addressing cultural problems

In one organisation I worked in, the cultural problem was clear at an early stage. The annual engagement survey wasn't great, but more than that, the mood and vibe of the place were negative, defensive, and unhelpful. 'It's in the walls,' remarked one staff member.

Significant environmental issues contributed to the current climate, including poor organisational processes, lack of organisational justice and distinct group hierarchy and competitiveness rather than cohesion and workgroups aligned to achieve the organisational outcomes. There were high levels of disengagement and organisational cynicism and a high percentage of technical leaders with no formal leadership training.

I was newly appointed to head up the People and Culture division, and I saw an opportunity when the latest engagement survey results hit my table. Previously, only summary versions of the engagement survey results were communicated to staff. Rarely had any of the findings resulted in any meaningful change. As a result, staff were ambivalent about the survey process or any hope of action.

I wanted to change that. At the very least, I wanted transparency of results at the leadership team meetings. This was important if I was to earn this group's trust.

In change, we need to show people why this change will be different from previous attempts.

I did that. I said, here are the results. Here are the themes. Here are the concern areas. Now I want to work with you to co-create a strategy to address the issues. This had never happened before. Not the transparency, the intent, or the co-creation.

I scheduled a series of workshops and shared my plans on how this would occur. We made the workshops optional, invited candour by excluding the CEO and senior executive, and were blown away when the first workshop attracted nearly total attendance.

Given the levels of disengagement, I'd been ready for humiliation if no one showed. At every workshop, almost every leader attended. They were not only present, but they were also active, interested and contributing positively to designing their future state culture.

Here's what I did.

Step 1: Consultation

Rather than design a series of behaviours and impose them, I invited all of the people leaders in for a series of co-design workshops.

In the lead up to the invitation, I was transparent with the survey results and showed genuine interest in understanding their challenges and frustrations, which they respected.

More than anything, they were thrilled to have the problems aired rather than swept under the table and to have an opportunity to contribute to and co-design the new culture and behaviours. They wanted to have a voice.

I intentionally asked the CEO and directors not to attend the workshops. The groups needed to discuss their concerns openly.

A few pockets of less-than-constructive debriefing were necessary to move forward on a long history of challenges, but most of the discussion was solution-focused. There was a sense of hope and optimism in the group that I'd not previously witnessed.

Step 2: Define the problem

I tabled the responses to the survey and my observations in a presentation before the first co-design workshop. I presented what I saw as the problems causing the cultural challenges and how the survey results confirmed them. Then, I asked them to challenge or validate the evidence.

Step 3: Co-create the solutions

I established five working tables with each of the main concern themes. Groups rotated across these tables during the first half-day workshop.

Individuals went first to the table that held the theme they were most interested in or concerned about. They used templates I'd prepared that asked them to identify the current state of the problem, give examples and describe the impact. Then they brainstormed solutions for moving forward.

I was realistic upfront about what could be achieved and said we were looking at a three-year transformation program.

They didn't care and celebrated that everything would be captured in a plan with visibility over progress. For the first time, many expressed optimism that things would change.

Step 4: Collate and regroup

My fabulous assistant collected hundreds of sheets of paper and scrawled-on templates and typed them into a manageable document across the theme areas. We placed this on a shared drive and invited all participants to review and contribute to the draft before the final workshop.

Many did. Many did not. I was happy with the response rate, given the demands on people's time.

The important action here was the transparency and opportunity to contribute.

Step 5: Final review and priority actions

In the last workshop, we tabled the final document that encompassed all feedback received in Step 4.

Groups were then asked to agree on priority actions for the next twelve months. This achieved three things. It made it very clear that change takes time. It reinforced a commitment to addressing all of the issues raised but indicated they would need to be prioritised and addressed in order of urgency that they would set. And finally, it made them discuss and agree on their biggest problems.

That brought quick momentum and respect from the leadership group when they could see us actively progressing a priority item. It also stopped any criticism or negativity if particular issues were not advanced immediately.

The final outcomes were incorporated into a broader People and Culture Action Plan that was reworked to address cultural concerns and leadership actions. All these actions formed part of a broader cultural vision for the organisation.

The outcome

The transparency led to a boost in engagement survey completion rates because people could see the results were regarded seriously, and actions were taken, not ignored.

We created a compelling change plan for people and culture that was aspirational, inspirational *and* achievable, co-designed with the leadership group.

Our positive actions also boosted the culture in other pockets or sub-cultures of the organisation.

But. (You knew this was coming, didn't you? It was too good to be true!)

The main barrier to culture transformation for this organisation was the devolved attitude that considered culture as something like a separate work task or project. One that only HR was responsible for, rather than enabling complete organisational performance, efficiency, safety and success.

It was also easily disposed of or put aside when other organisational pressures mounted.

Despite that, this case study shows how easy it can be to re-engage a disengaged group and strengthen culture through simple acts of transparency, positive intent, and co-creation.

And perhaps this case study reinforces the important role executives play in leading systemic change in their organisations. They need to take active ownership of culture, not devolve it. To recognise culture as the only enabler of organisational performance and give due and appropriate attention to building and nurturing it.

> 'We all need to be the cultural architects of our workplace.'

As Timothy Clark says, 'We all need to be the cultural architects of our workplace.'

Chapter Summary

We are all cultural architects of our workplace.

We can use sub-cultures to influence positive change locally if we can't influence systemic change from the top. This is not as sustainable but avoids destroying the hopes of passionate change leaders.

Culture is the enabler of organisational success, and our people are our most valuable asset.

Culture is not like yoghurt; we don't set and forget it.

When fixing a toxic culture, recruiting to the new desired culture is not the first step.

Transparency of engagement survey results is essential for getting buy-in to transformation activities.

If all else fails, don't be afraid to be that lone nut.

Be realistic about timeframes and efforts when transforming culture.

Taking Action

Assess your current state of culture. Is remediation required?

Define your future state culture. What does it look like? How are people acting in this future state? How do they feel about coming to work each day?

What changes do you need to make to get to your future state culture?

Co-create the vision with existing employees, drawing on engagement results or feedback as the catalyst for the change. Communicate why things will be different this time.

What Actions Will You Take?

1. _____

2. _____

3. _____

Chapter Thirteen

Safe and Effective Leadership

'We need leaders not in love with money,
but in love with justice. Not in love with
publicity, but in love with humanity.'
— Dr Martin Luther King Jr

Safe and effective leadership is about influencing and leading for positive actions and outcomes rather than personal gain. These leaders are ethical and integral to transforming into a mentally healthy workplace.

In this chapter, you'll learn about the six traits of safe and effective leadership and how to build the necessary leadership skills into your capability frameworks to ensure your mentally healthy workplace is sustainable.

Leading for a new norm

It is essential to equip leaders with the appropriate skills and knowledge to lead safely and effectively in a modern workplace. Leaders must be clear on their understanding of leadership instead of management and understand the power of their actions and behaviours in promoting a positive and safe workplace culture or potentially contributing to psychological harm.

A common practice in workplaces is promoting employees into leadership roles due to technical competencies or tenure rather than leadership capabilities or potential.

> Ensure you are managing tasks and leading people.

Promoting for technical abilities or tenure is completely reasonable and a lovely recognition of efforts and skills — as long as a leadership training and coaching program accompanies the step up, there have been no behaviour concerns, and the individual has sound interpersonal skills.

Sadly, we still see individuals promoted to leadership roles for productivity over people skills.

Leadership versus management

If you hold responsibility for people, you will have both a managerial and a leadership component to your role. The key is to ensure you are managing tasks and leading people.

Managing tasks include:

- rostering
- leave approvals
- budgeting
- planning
- resourcing.

These are functions you *manage*, but when it comes to people — you *lead*.

A leader:

- positively influences
- sets the vision for the team
- provides clarity on roles and responsibilities
- sets individual and team goals that align with organisational strategy
- provides recognition, reward and appropriate feedback
- motivates and mobilises, and
- monitors wellbeing and engagement.

True leadership isn't about getting accolades or wielding power or authority, although that outdated mindset is still carried by many.

Leadership is an ongoing journey of personal growth. There is no endpoint, no finalised knowledge where you can say, 'That's it. I'm done. I'm a leader now'. There will continue to be challenges and changes and the need for constant self-reflection and growth.

Good leaders recognise this. Good leaders are open to change. Good leaders know that leadership is a privilege, not a position.

The six traits of safe and effective leaders

Leadership is a discipline and a profession that needs nurturing.

The following six traits are evident in safe and effective leaders. They mitigate common work-related stress factors, increase individual and team performance, and ensure that reasonable management actions are clear and taken according to legislative principles.

The latter is important. Firstly, to avoid any serious failure of due process, and secondly, to ensure that poor performance in any individual is promptly addressed before it permeates other team members.

These traits are covered in detail in my *Six Traits of Safe and Effective Leaders* training program[53] and will be the sole topic of my next book providing specific guidance for leaders.

The *Six Traits* program recognises that safe and effective leaders:

- clarify roles, responsibilities, and expectations
- communicate and care effectively
- support teams to understand and resolve conflict
- enable contributions from all team members
- coach for accountability and empowerment, and
- monitor and correct actions promptly and fairly.

In addition, to transform the norm and create and sustain mentally healthy workplaces, leaders must develop the following skills and knowledge:

- a basic understanding of psychological safety
- awareness of common work-related stress factors and how to address them, and
- knowledge of change management principles and why people may resist workplace change.

Leaders need to support their teams to develop and grow. And importantly, leaders must accept that supporting their team to develop and grow and manage the challenges of a modern workplace is a core component of their role.

Let's explore each of the traits briefly.

Clarify roles, responsibilities and expectations

Lack of clarity of roles, responsibilities, priorities and expectations is a work-related stress factor. The leader's job is to ensure that team members are clear on their role, their specific functions and areas of responsibility (including delegation authority) and continually communicate changes.

Clarifying responsibilities and expectations also includes being clear on timelines and assisting team members in reprioritising if there are competing demands, and keeping an eye on work volume.

Communicate and care effectively

At times, leaders are so bogged down with operational duties they forget that a core part of leadership is communicating and caring for the individuals on their team.

> Things start to crumble when people don't feel supported.

It can be tempting to knuckle down or hide away from the team to get work done. This is completely reasonable for short chunks of protected time where you have communicated it appropriately. But not being present, not being visible or checking in with your teams informally and formally is just poor leadership.

Alexandra Rowe says access to leaders for communication is important. While it may be challenging to find time for adequate conversations with team members, it is an essential part of a leader's role. She says things start to crumble when people don't feel supported.

Caring effectively means taking steps to monitor the *wellbeing* of team members — not just their *outputs*.

Support teams to understand and resolve conflict

Chapter Five explored poor workplace relationships and the common causes of workplace conflict. Leaders need to support individuals in understanding how and why conflict arises and develop their ability to have constructive conversations to resolve tensions or disputes.

This may include training on assertiveness skills, providing constructive and supportive feedback rather than criticisms and always leading with the right intent.

The key here is for leaders to ensure they have these skills and then develop them in their teams.

A constructive and practical approach to conflict will minimise work-related stress risks around relationship breakdowns.

Enable contributions from all team members

In Chapter Three, we examined the concept of psychological safety and how this is necessary for building high performing teams. Encourage contributions from team members by openly inviting them to contribute, solve problems, and raise ideas or concerns. The unleashing potential model (figure 5) showed the difference between green and red light leaders. If we don't invite contributions or actively shut them down, we disengage employees and potentially increase their risk of psychological harm.

Leaders need every team member to feel safe to contribute.

In a recent coaching conversation, a client discussed the need for managers to take greater responsibility. She needed her team to run solutions by her for veto rather than bring problems for her to solve.

I asked if my client had ever given her managers permission to develop solutions. I wondered if she had specifically articulated that she wanted them to bring ideas and solutions and looked forward to their insights. She hadn't.

Sometimes team members just need to be given the green light. That may not be about your leadership but rather a hangover from a previous leader or workplace norm where they were not invited or encouraged to develop solutions.

All you need to do is explicitly ask and give them permission to contribute.

Coach for accountability and empowerment

Coaching can be misunderstood. It tends to be viewed as a corrective action to remedy a skill or behavioural issue. But coaching is about using clever questioning techniques to encourage people to reach their own answers. And in doing so, we empower them and increase their self-belief.

A common workplace assumption is that leaders know how to coach their teams. How would they?

Coaching is a discipline. Most coaches, myself included, have undertaken extensive formal qualifications and conducted hundreds of hours of coaching to earn our credentials.

Who has supported leaders to do this?

Leaders should have a basic understanding of coaching concepts and be equipped with a repertoire of core coaching questions. One set of questions I provide most often are those required to build accountability and responsibility in team members.

A common scenario, particularly for new leaders, is that a team member will bring them a problem, metaphorically drop it in the leader's lap, say thanks very much, then jog off to their tea break. Meanwhile the leader crumbles under the mountain of other problems they're still working through.

Sometimes leaders can feel like it's their job to solve all the problems, or they believe it's easier than trying to hold a conversation and instil some accountability in the team member.

But it's not.

Develop people to think for themselves

It's your job to develop people to think for themselves and bring you solutions or suggestions, not to solve their problems for them.

How will they learn if you do that?

The other side of this coin is the importance of coaching rather than telling. Language such as 'Do this' or 'Try that' tells team members what they should do, rather than empowering them to think for themselves.

Use simple coaching questions such as: What have you tried so far? What else could you try? Who does know? What other steps could you take?

Supporting leaders with basic coaching knowledge will save them time, ensure they manage their workload effectively and build capacity in their teams.

Monitor and correct actions fairly and promptly

Have you ever worked hard in a team where one team member seemed to get away with murder or just didn't pull their weight?

What about a workplace where a staff member seems to behave appallingly, yet they are never pulled up for it?

Equip your leaders with the skills and knowledge to monitor, manage and correct performance in a way that aligns with due process, is within legislative guidelines and confidently allows them to hold people to account. Apply this right across the organisation.

When processes are inconsistently applied, or industrial action is sought and a disciplinary outcome is overturned, leaders can lose confidence (or hope) that their efforts to address poor behaviours are worth it.

Seeking expert advice is often recommended when understanding performance management processes for someone with a disclosed mental illness. Leaders can be extremely vulnerable in these situations. Appropriate support ensures that poor or inappropriate performance or behaviours are not left unaddressed, impacting other team members or the broader workplace.

By giving your leaders the ability to monitor and correct actions fairly and promptly, you will hold the line on behavioural expectations and have leaders confidently performing their duties.

Leadership capability framework

Think about the safe and effective leadership traits essential for your leaders in a mentally healthy workplace. Do you have a leadership capability framework in place, or are you developing one? Does your framework encompass all or any of the traits mentioned above?

Have your leaders received training in psychological safety to foster inclusion and learner safety and encourage contributions from their team? Are your leaders skilled in the basic principles of change management? Can they recognise the difference between change management and project management? Do they understand why poorly managed change is such a significant contributor to work-related stress?

When developing or updating your leadership capability frameworks, look to the future to ensure your leaders are supported and equipped to lead safely and effectively.

The leader's role in reducing stigma

Mental health is about wellness rather than illness. It is not merely the absence of a mental health condition, rather, it exists on a continuum from positive, healthy functioning to severe daily impact. We move along this continuum in response to work and life events and individual circumstances.

In that way, it is similar to physical wellbeing.

When leaders hold regular check-in chats with their employees, one of their concerns is whether they're expected to take on the role of counsellor.

During a coaching session, an executive asked about the line between showing care and concern and being overly invested in individuals. He knew one of his people was struggling and wanted to extend support. He'd provided details of the EAP service to the employee but wasn't sure if he should be doing more.

My guidance was simple. Ask, 'Is there anything I can do to help or support you right now?'

There is absolutely no expectation for you to counsel employees. Stay within your role scope but show the same care and concern you would if an employee had a physical injury.

Ask, 'How can we best accommodate you right now?' 'What can we do to help you?'

Leaders are understandably uncertain of their role in these situations and can feel a little insecure. One of the best ways to address this is to roll out a Mental Health First Aid program across the workplace. Some organisations have started this at executive or people-leader level, while others extended an open invitation for anyone to attend.

I know of some organisations that have established a panel of Mental Health First Aiders — much like their physical health counterparts. They are responsible for reducing the stigma, promoting information and education and ensuring relevant supportive strategies and services are fostered within the organisation.

Leaders will build skills and confidence, and the workplace will actively reduce the stigma around mental wellbeing. That should make regular check-ins easier, with less pressure or expectations of leaders being counsellors.

Other ways to reduce the stigma in the workplace include storytelling and leadership modelling and normalising language around monitoring and looking after psychological wellbeing. Beyond Blue, along with WorkSafe Victoria, has created extensive resources to promote mental health in the workplace and reduce associated stigmas.

Chapter Summary

Leadership is a discipline, a profession that needs nurturing. There is no endpoint, only further discoveries about yourself and those you lead.

Safe and effective leaders mitigate work-related stress factors, increase individual and team performance and ensure reasonable management actions accord with legislative principles.

The six traits of safe and effective leaders are essential, along with the three fundamental skills and knowledge areas of psychological safety, common work-related stress risks and change management.

Leadership capability frameworks should encompass these core skills.

Our mental health exists on a continuum much like our physical health.

Leaders have a role in monitoring the psychological wellbeing of their employees – not counselling or diagnosing.

Mental Health First Aid training can equip all people in the workplace with core skills and the confidence to have a conversation with someone they are concerned about.

Taking Action

Develop a leadership capability/competency framework for your workplace that includes the six traits and the three knowledge areas.

Ensure monthly structured 1:1 conversations are taking place and include a wellbeing component. Download a template from my website to help with this www.tanyaheaneyvoogt. com/resources.

Ensure leaders are trained in reasonable management actions.

Undertake strengths-based coaching with leaders to help them understand their natural strengths and blind spots. Provide coaching on areas that prevent them from leading safely and effectively and may derail your transformation efforts.

Have a strong focus on promoting or recruiting for culture and productivity.

Promote the mental health continuum and the notion that mental wellbeing is akin to physical wellbeing.

Train or coach managers to recognise when their people are struggling and have conversations with those they are concerned about.

Display posters about mental wellbeing to normalise it.

Open up conversations about mental wellbeing by asking, 'How are you travelling?'

What Actions Will You Take?

1. _____

2. _____

3. _____

Chapter Fourteen

Leading the Change

'When you are up to your neck in alligators, it's
hard to think about draining the swamp.'
— John Litt

Several years ago, I sat face-to-face with a People and Culture executive to discuss creating a mentally healthy workplace.

He was full of positive intent and armed with the knowledge and everyday issues that reinforced the need to do this work. And he was at his wit's end. He had struggled to get out of the weeds and into the strategy. He struggled even to review the amount of information available on this topic. Information overload is a problem in itself.

Throwing the Beyond Blue pack across the desk with an anguished look, he pleaded, 'Can you help me?!'

So began my journey with this client to transform their workplace. It's a long game. They were shaking off a challenging history and some entrenched cultural challenges.

In a training room with workplace change advocates, we set about co-designing the strategy. They had expressed their dissatisfaction with the organisation. They were frustrated that they had brought forward ideas and suggestions and gave their time to lead some of the work, but nothing had changed. Yet the simple act of bringing them together to inform the strategic action plan rejuvenated this group of dedicated, talented employees.

Within six months of launching the Mentally Healthy Workplaces Strategic Action Plan, responses to their annual employee survey showed a thirty-seven per cent lift in the questions about work-related stress and the organisation's psychological wellbeing support.

The simple step of recognising, acting and communicating the intent to focus on transitioning to a mentally healthy workplace gave employees hope and a sense of optimism that things would change.

It has been one of my most significant learnings in all the years I've been implementing this work. The early wins bring renewed energy and engagement — purely from announcing your intention and demonstrating that you take this transformation seriously.

In this chapter, I want to prepare you to lead the change. I have listed the questions you need to answer first and will detail the people you need to engage and help lead the change to a mentally healthy workplace.

But first. You have a choice to make.

Will you continue to fight off the alligators, or will you take that first step to drain the swamp?

Start with why

Before embarking on any communication or discussions, you need to be very clear on why this change matters. Without that understanding, the initiative will likely fail.

You may have been reading, researching and thinking about ways to lead this change for some time. Perhaps you have already mapped out the steps to progress towards the future state and are impatient to get cracking and move people along.

You understand the reasons and are moving forward. But when you start conversations, you'll need to provide the appropriate context and bring others up to speed.

You need to help them move off the starting line.

Remember, they are not where you are with your thinking, so you need to help them move off the starting line.

Develop meaningful responses to the following questions *before* you start communicating.

Why are we embarking on the journey to become a mentally healthy workplace?

Why is this important and a priority for us now? (Particularly given other activities we are working on.)

How will we be supported to make the required changes? What resources, training and support will we have?

What happens if we don't change?

What happens if we do?

Successful communication hinges on a 'why' that is compelling to the audience, not just you. Talking about meeting compliance requirements or addressing OHS risks probably won't engage many people. Build your messages to suit your audiences and make sure there's a strong 'What's in it for me' message for them.

Plan

What story is your data telling you?

What are the people feeling/saying/doing?

What is the mood/vibe/climate of your workplace?

Is there much interpersonal conflict?

What are some compelling reasons for transforming into a mentally healthy workplace? Think about the different perspectives you need to influence in your change work.

What does success look like for you?

How will you know when you have achieved your future state?

How will you monitor uptake and utilisation of the new ways of working?

How will you ensure you don't take your foot off the accelerator too soon?

Where do you currently sit on the mentally healthy workplace maturity model? (See Chapter One, this is your current state.)

What steps do you need to take to move along the transformational continuum? Plan one step at a time to avoid overwhelm.

Seek to understand the specifics of your change project.

How large is the change gap? Are you moving from a superficial approach, or have you already had a business case approved?

What and who will be impacted by the changes? Both in rolling out the change initiatives and in receiving and adopting them?

Are the changes minor, or do they require a shift in values, beliefs, attitudes, and behaviours? The latter is most common with this type of work.

Who will be involved in the change management project? Who will be on your change team?

What skills do they need to implement the change?

How will you support them?

Answer these questions fully to establish robust processes and support mechanisms to lead this change.

The change team

Successful organisational change (that enhances, not detracts, from culture) is rarely led by one person. In larger organisations, we see a triangle arrangement, with an executive sponsor, a project lead and a change lead.

All three roles are essential. In larger organisations, they can be different people or different teams.

In small to medium-sized organisations, the change leader is often the project leader; and, in rare circumstances, also the executive sponsor.

We refer to this group as our change team.

Alongside the team, we need to build a change coalition that includes executives, managers and leaders, and change champions who will help us roll out the required changes.

Who is the executive sponsor of your change project?

How will they communicate about the change?

Will they actively support and champion the change ahead?

Will they help recruit other executives to support the change?

Do they understand the need to remain visible and supportive of this project for the duration and beyond?

Which other executives, managers and leaders will support the change and be in your change coalition?

Change champions

Selecting the right people to be your change champions is vital. Ideally, recruit them from all functional areas at varying levels of the organisation. They should be influencers in your workplace, but it's not about authority or title; they are popular and respected by their peers.

Given what you know about the change project and these people, who might be vocal supporters?

Sometimes this will mean having a personal conversation and requesting their help to spread positive messages about the change. Approach them directly and help them see what role they can play.

Don't cut the ribbon and run

While there's a temptation for busy executives sponsoring change to cut the ribbon and run, it's vital to maintain genuine interest and visible support throughout and, in many cases, well after the initiative.

What this looks like may vary depending on the breadth, depth and complexity of your change. However, this ongoing high-level sponsorship is essential when discussing such transformational work.

Executive sponsors will require support to understand the importance of their role, and change leaders will need to help them undertake necessary tasks.

The salami in the change sandwich

Middle managers are an integral part, as they are instrumental in driving the change forward through their direct reports. Despite this, middle managers are often left out of discussions or consultations and then given the unenviable task of having to sell the message down the line.

> Engage with your middle managers from the outset.

This is unfair and unhelpful. And it most certainly will not help to engage or motivate this crucial group of personnel. Engage with your middle managers from the outset. Ask for their ideas and support. Invite them to co-design actions for your strategic action plan and keep them active and informed.

You will also need to support them to coach their direct reports through change. Consider what training they may need here.

Equip them with the responses to your 'why' questions outlined earlier in this chapter. They need to clearly and confidently share the business reasons with their direct reports. When asked why the change is a priority, the answer is not that it's a legislative requirement.

Don't take the easy road here. Spend time cultivating different messages to share with different audiences. Develop a messaging guide for the entire duration of your project, then arm your middle managers with these messages and ensure their thorough understanding and belief.

Communication

Change communications differ from regular organisational communications in that the messages and activities are specifically designed to help people transition through the stages.

Everything about your messaging is strategic. It can either enhance your success in transitioning people or create further obstacles, resistance and disaffection.

> Everything about your messaging is strategic.

Show and ask instead of telling. Cleverly script choices for the readers or provide information that helps reduce barriers.

Be transparent and share what you know, ensuring you get messages out promptly before the rumour mill hits and messages are distorted.

Chapter Summary

In the face of incessant business-as-usual demands, it is tempting to delay the proactive work to transform your workplace norms. Don't. Focus on draining the swamp.

Plan your approach and the steps needed to traverse the maturity continuum. Answering the questions in the Plan section will help you prepare for and successfully lead this work.

Bring others with you. Take the time to set the scene and offer a compelling case, so they'll feel as passionate about this work as you do and support the change initiatives.

Taking Action

Review your current state on the mentally healthy workplace maturity model.

Answer the questions in the Plan section.

Strategically identify the people at the change party.

Develop your compelling 'why' and communicate this well ahead of any action.

Use your mentally healthy workplaces working party to help influence change.

If you are resource-lean, reach out for professional change support to navigate this space.

What Actions Will You Take?

1. _____

2. _____

3. _____

Conclusion

Don't Wait for the Alligators to Stop Circling

William James said it well. 'It is our attitude at the beginning of a difficult task which, more than anything else, will affect its successful outcome.'

There will never be a perfect time to start this work.

The longer you put it off, the wider the change gap and potential remediation work required. As we heard from Georgie Chapman and Alexandra Rowe in earlier chapters, the biggest risk is for organisations with their heads in the sand that resist taking any action.

This book has given you a storehouse of strategies. You are now aware of the most common psychological harm risks and ways to prevent or mitigate these.

You have detailed information on how to lead successful workplace change and how to design, reinforce and nurture a positive workplace culture. And you have a step-by-step approach to introducing and reinforcing psychological safety in your workplace.

Working through the Plan questions in the final chapter will ensure you are appropriately prepared to communicate and start leading your change to a mentally healthy workplace.

Transforming outdated norms is not for the faint-hearted. This work takes courage, empathy, and sheer determination.

I continue to be moved, inspired, and reassured by the number of well-meaning individuals I meet who are passionate about this transformative work. This book is for all leaders of positive workplace change who strive to make workplaces happier, healthier places. Thank you for the role you play.

About the Author

Tanya Heaney-Voogt is a mentally healthy workplaces expert, workplace change facilitator and certified leadership coach. She helps leaders, teams and organisations to thrive in this rapidly changing and high demand world of work.

With a twenty-five-year career leading people, projects and change across the health sector, Tanya now works primarily with public sector entities.

Drawing on her experience as a senior leader dealing with work overload and change saturation, Tanya supports leaders in developing more sustainable individual strategies and assists workplaces in managing the environmental factors that contribute to unsafe levels of work-related stress.

Her engaging and authentic approach is always remarked upon as she brings life to her content, helping people absorb essential information and implement strategies to achieve real change.

Tanya has worked extensively with health, education, local government and environmental agencies in consulting, coaching and training activities, including her popular *Cracking the Change Code*™ program. This blended program has supported many public entities in implementing enterprise-wide change initiatives. The program ensures change leaders develop the necessary skills and knowledge to lead successful change safely and effectively into the future.

The *Transforming Norm*™ workplace transformation program aligns with the content in this book. It combines a series of support activities into a holistic transformation program, making it easier for workplaces to become mentally healthy.

Tanya lives in the rolling hills of Gippsland, Victoria. When not working diligently in her practice (or on her next book), she can be found dining out with her husband, the beloved Mr V, enjoying a drive through the hills or laughing with family and friends.

You can find out more about Tanya's programs and services, read her blogs and access free downloadable resources on her website www.tanyaheaneyvoogt.com

Tanya loves to hear from people who are passionate about building mentally healthy workplaces. She invites you to connect via LinkedIn or email.

LinkedIn: www.linkedin.com/in/tanyaheaneyvoogt/

Email: tanya@tanyaheaneyvoogt.com

Current Research

In recognition of the evolving nature of workplace psychological health and safety and my continual research in this space, a current list of research links and guidance material is maintained on the resources section of my website www.tanyaheaneyvoogt.com

Endnotes

1. National Academies of Sciences, Engineering, and Medicine; Division of Behavioral and Social Sciences and Education; Health and Medicine Division; Committee on Law and Justice; Board on Children, Youth, and Families; Board on Global Health. (2018 Apr 6). *Forum on Global Violence Prevention.* Addressing the Social and Cultural Norms That Underlie the Acceptance of Violence: Proceedings of a Workshop — in Brief. National Academies Press. https://www.ncbi.nlm.nih.gov/books/NBK493719/

2. Australian Government Productivity Commission. (2020). *Inquiry Report Mental Health* (p. 11). https://www.pc.gov.au/inquiries/completed/mental-health/report/mental-health.pdf

3. Australian Government Productivity Commission. (2020). *Inquiry Report Mental Health* (p. 295). https://www.pc.gov.au/inquiries/completed/mental-health/report/mental-health.pdf

4. Towell, N. (2021). Workers' Mental Health Claims Help Put WorkCover Back in the Red. *The Age.* https://www.theage.com.au/national/victoria/workers-mental-health-claims-help-put-workcover-back-in-the-red-20210624-p583sp.html

5. Victorian Workplace Mental Wellbeing Collaboration. (2018). *What works to promote workplace wellbeing:*

A rapid review of recent policy developments and intervention research (pp. 6, 11-29). Victoria.

6. National Mental Health Commission. (2014). *Developing a mentally healthy workplace: A review of the literature* (pp. 11-62). Australian Government.

7. The Change Lab. (2020). *The State of Change in Australian Workplaces* (p. 12). https://www.michellemcquaid.com/product/the-change-lab-2020-workplace-survey-report/

8. SuperFriend. (2021). *Indicators of a Thriving Workplace National Report 2021*. https://itw2021.superfriend.com.au/

9. Victorian State Government. (2020). *Victorian Recorded Crime Statistics*. https://www.crimestatistics.vic.gov.au/media-centre/news/media-release-decreases-in-high-volume-property-offences-offset-by-the

10. NSW Health. (2020). *What factors can affect behaviour? Principles for effective support*. https://www.health.nsw.gov.au/mentalhealth/psychosocial/principles/Pages/behaviour-factors.aspx

11. Leader Factor. (2020). *What is Psychological Safety?* https://www.leaderfactor.com/psychological-safety

12. Edmondson, A. (2019). *The Fearless Organization*. John Wiley & Sons.

13. Ibid.

14. Google. (2016). *Understand Team Effectiveness*. https://rework.withgoogle.com/guides/understanding-team-effectiveness/steps/introduction/

15. Pellerin, C. (2009). *How NASA Builds Teams*. John Wiley & Sons (pp. 3-12).

16. Johnson, D. (2008). Success, Failure, and NASA Culture. *ASK Magazine*. https://appel.nasa.gov/2008/09/01/success-failure-and-nasa-culture/

17. Clark, T. (2020). *The 4 Stages of Psychological Safety*. Berrett-Koehler Publishers.

18. Cazaly, L. (2019). *Ish* (5th ed.).

19. Gallwey, W. T. (2015). *The Inner Game of Tennis*. Pan Macmillan.

20. Edmondson, A. (2019). *The Fearless Organization*. John Wiley & Sons.

21. de Bono, E. (1999). *Six Thinking Hats: Run better meetings, make faster decisions*. Penguin Random House UK.

22. Have your say NSW. (2021). *Tell us what you think about a Psychological Health Code of Practice*. https://www.haveyoursay.nsw.gov.au/draft-code-psychological-health

23. NSW Government Safe Work. (2021). *Code of Practice: Managing psychosocial hazards at work*.

24. Towell, N. (2021). *Workers' Mental Health Claims Help Put WorkCover Back in the Red*. The Age. https://www.theage.com.au/national/victoria/workers-mental-health-claims-help-put-workcover-back-in-the-red-20210624-p583sp.html

25. WorkSafe. (2022). *Proposed Occupational Health and Safety Amendment (Psychological Health) Regulations.* https://engage.vic.gov.au/proposed-psychological-health-regulations

26. Karasek, R. & Theorell, T. (1992). *Healthy work stress, productivity and the reconstruction of working life.* Basic Books.

27. Fraser, A. (2020). *Strive.* John Wiley & Sons Australia.

28. NBC. (2018). New Amsterdam [TV programme].

29. Manheimer, E. (2012). *Twelve Patients.* Grand Central Publishing.

30. Hall, D. (2021). 8 negative micro-behaviours that HR should address. *HRM.* Australian HR Institute. https://www.hrmonline.com.au/culture/micro-behaviours-workplace/

31. Wintle, J. (2019). Workplace Civility; How do you do? *Steople.* https://www.steople.com.au/civility/

32. Schmidt, L. (2018) Workplace civility doesn't just remedy burnout, it saves lives. *HRM.* Australian HR Institute. https://www.hrmonline.com.au/section/featured/remedy-burnout-civility/

33. Hofstede Insights. (2022). *National Culture.* https://hi.hofstede-insights.com/national-culture.

34. Neilson, K. (2020). Are you really having a bad day? Or did you catch it from your colleague? *HRM.* Australian HR Institute. https://www.hrmonline.com.au/behaviour/emotional-contagion-workplace/

35. Chamine, S. (2016). *Positive intelligence: Why only 20% of teams and individuals achieve their true potential and how you can achieve yours.* Greenleaf Book Group Press.

36. Diversity Council Australia. (2021). *DCA Inclusion@ Work Index 2021-2022: Mapping the State of Inclusion in the Australian Workforce.*

37. Diversity Council Australia. (2021). *The Australian Business Case for Diversity and Inclusion.* https:// www.dca.org.au/inclusion-at-work-index/australian-business-case-di

38. Victorian Auditor-General's Office. (2016). *Bullying and Harassment in the Health Sector.*

39. Worksafe.vic.gov.au. *Workplace bullying risk indicator.* https://www.worksafe.vic.gov.au/resources/ workplace-bullying-risk-indicator

40. Victorian Auditor-General's Office. (2016). *Bullying and Harassment in the Health Sector Report.* https://www. audit.vic.gov.au/sites/default/files/20160323-Bullying. pdf

41. Williamson, S. (2022). Andrew Laming: why empathy training is unlikely to work. *The Conversation.* https:// theconversation.com/andrew-laming-why-empathy-training-is-unlikely-to-work-158050

42. Peterson, K. & McCleery E. (2014). *Evidence Brief: The Effectiveness of Mandatory Computer-Based Trainings on Government Ethics, Workplace Harassment, Or Privacy And Information Security-Related Topics.* Department

of Veterans Affairs, Health Services Research & Development Services. https://www.ncbi.nlm.nih. gov/books/NBK384612/pdf/Bookshelf_NBK384612. pdf

43. Dobbin, F. & Kalev, A. (2016). Why Diversity Programs Fail. *Harvard Business Review.* https://hbr. org/2016/07/why-diversity-programs-fail.

44. Berger, J. (2020). *The Catalyst: How to change anyone's mind.* Simon & Schuster UK.

45. Harvard.edu. (2022). *Frank Dobbin.* https://scholar. harvard.edu/dobbin/home

46. Prosci. (2022). Why Change Management. *Prosci.* https://www.prosci.com/resources/articles/why-change-management

47. Horlick, A. 6 Strategies for Reducing Change Saturation. *Prosci.* https://blog.prosci.com/6-strategies-for-reducing-change-saturation

48. Deal, T. & Kennedy, A. (1982). *Corporate cultures.* Addison-Wesley.

49. Department of Treasury and Finance, Victorian State Government. (2016). *Asset Management Accountability Framework.*

50. Kotter, J. (2012). *Leading Change.* Harvard Business School Press.

51. Leisure Networks. (2022). *Who are we.* Leisure Networks. https://www.leisurenetworks.org/who-are-we/

52. Sivers, D. (2010, Feb). *How to start a movement.* [Video]. Ted Conferences. https://www.ted.com/ talks/derek_sivers_how_to_start_a_movement

53. Heaney-Voogt, T. (2019). *Programs — Tanya Heaney-Voogt.* Tanya Heaney-Voogt. https://tanyaheaneyvoogt. com/programs/.

www.ingramcontent.com/pod-product-compliance
Lightning Source LLC
Chambersburg PA
CBHW071200210326
41597CB00016B/1622